Anger Management in Schools

Alternatives to
Student Violence

Second Edition

Jerry Wilde

A SCARECROWEDUCATION BOOK

The Scarecrow Press, Inc.
Lanham, Maryland, and Oxford
2002

A ScarecrowEducation Book

Published in the United States of America
by Scarecrow Press, Inc.
4720 Boston Way, Lanham, Maryland 20706
www.scarecrowpress.com

12 Hid's Copse Road
Cumnor Hill, Oxford OX2 9JJ, England

British Library Cataloguing in Publication Information Available

Library of Congress Cataloging-in-Publication Data

Wilde, Jerry, 1962-
    Anger management in schools : alternatives to student violence / Jerry
Wilde.— 2nd ed.
        p. cm.
    "A ScarecrowEducation book."
    Includes bibliographical references and index.
    ISBN 0-8108-4209-2 (pbk. : alk. paper)
    ISBN 0-8108-4476-1 (alk. paper)
    1. School violence—Prevention. 2. Rational-emotive psychotherapy.
    3. Anger in children. I. Title.
LB3013.3 .W55 2002
371.4′6—dc21

                                                                2002002137

Contents

1   The Interaction of Anger and Violence in Schools: The Costs to Learning   1

2   Hostility and Health: The Relationship between Anger, Stress, and Illness   9

3   Characteristics of Angry and Aggressive Students   13

4   Two Opposing Theories on the Cause of Anger in Children and Adolescents   27

5   The Differences between REBT and Other Approaches   45

6   Setting the Stage for Change   59

7   Techniques for Coping with Anger   69

8   Depression, Anger, and Aggression   101

9   Transcriptions   107

10   Anger Control Groups and Classroom Lessons   123

11   Additional Anger Management Techniques   155

12   Strategies for Keeping Students Safe   163

13   School-Wide Safety Assessment   171

14   Final Thoughts   177

Appendixes   179

Bibliography   187

Index   193

About the Author   195

The Interaction of Anger and Violence in Schools: The Costs to Learning

> One of the most significant problems facing our nation's schools is violence. In the past few years, violent crime by children and adolescents has risen dramatically. Murder and assault are becoming alarmingly common as it seems nearly every time an evening news cast airs there is a report regarding youth violence.
>
> —Wilde, *Anger Management in Schools*

This was the opening paragraph of the first edition of this book, *Anger Management in Schools: Alternatives to Student Violence.* It was written prior to the tragedies in Littleton (Columbine), Colorado; Paducah, Kentucky; Pearl, Mississippi; and Jonesboro, Arkansas. Sadly, the list could go on and on. According to the National School Safety Center (1997), nearly three million crimes occur in or near schools each year.

Anger and violence in our nation's schools have become a much more serious problem since the publication of the first edition of this book. Random acts of violence seem to have spread to most cities in the United States. Now no community, regardless of its location, is immune from life-threatening acts of violence and mayhem.

One of the factors associated with the rise of youth violence is the availability of guns. Adolescents can acquire a gun if they have the financial means. Guns may not have added to the frequency of violence, but they have certainly increased the severity of the results. If adolescents had a dispute a few years ago, the confrontation may have ended in some type of altercation; now, rather than a bloody nose, resolution may come in a hail of bullets.

Another change in youth violence has to do with the age of the offender. Previously, most of the violent incidents were perpetrated by older adolescents (sixteen and above). Now it is all too common for young children to be responsible for life-threatening assaults. The number of juvenile arrests in the United States increased 26 percent between 1980 and 1995. Arrests involving juveniles aged twelve or younger grew by 24 percent, and those involving juveniles aged thirteen and fourteen increased 54 percent (U.S. Department of Education and U.S. Department of Justice, 1999).

On March 24, 1998, Mitchell Johnson (age thirteen) and Andrew Golden (age eleven) pulled a fire alarm and opened fire on classmates and teachers evacuating the school building. The students were armed with three rifles and seven hand guns. The end result was the death of four students and a teacher, who died protecting a child. An eleven-year-old is typically not a threat to life and limb, but add a gun to the mix and the story changes completely.

There was an incident at an elementary school where I worked in which a fourth-grade boy held a piece of broken glass to the throat of a girl during recess. A few weeks later, a third-grader brought a switchblade to school in his backpack. He said some older boys had been picking on him on his way to school and he needed the knife for protection. A middle school student brought a gun to school recently. Let me add that these incidents did not take place in New York or Los Angeles; all of this occurred in a small town in rural Wisconsin with only 1,700 students in kindergarten through twelfth grade.

Having worked as an educational psychologist in three states at several elementary, middle, and high schools (both public and private), I have come to one inescapable conclusion, which many of you also may have reached: *There are no completely safe schools or communities.* The epidemic of violence can happen anywhere.

If you need more evidence, consider some statistics from the 1999 edition of the *Youth Risk Behavior Survey* (YRBS). This survey is given each year to high school students in all fifty states and, as the name suggests, focuses on behaviors that will affect the well-being of our nation's youth, such as alcohol and drug use, suicide, violence, and even preventative factors such as diet and exercise. The 1999 edition revealed the following facts:

- Some 17.3 percent of students had carried a weapon (i.e., a gun, knife, or club) in school at least once in the thirty days preceding the survey.

- Some 4.9 percent of students had carried a gun in school at least once in the thirty days preceding the survey.
- A total of 35.7 percent of students had been in a physical fight at least once in the twelve months preceding the survey (44 percent for males, 27.3 percent for females).
- Another 5.2 percent of students had missed at least one day of school in the preceding thirty days because they felt unsafe at school or when traveling to and from school.
- A total of 7.7 percent of students had been threatened with a weapon in the twelve months preceding the survey.

These statistics only measure observable instances of violence in the schools. Some of the other effects of anger and violence are less obvious but have more impact on the overall educational process. These "hidden effects" of anger and violence can be felt by every teacher and student in American schools.

A report entitled *Indicators of School Crime and Safety,* published by the U.S. Department of Education (National Center for Educational Statistics, 1998), confirmed what educators working in schools already suspected: Kids are increasingly worried about becoming a victim of violence while at school. The report highlighted these anxieties by reporting that in 1989 only 6 percent of students between the ages of twelve and nineteen feared they were going to be attacked or harmed at school. By 1995, that figure had increased to 9 percent. Between 1989 and 1995, the percentage of students who avoided one or more places at school fearing for their safety nearly doubled, increasing from 5 percent in 1989 to 9 percent in 1995. Between 1989 and 1995, the percentage of students who reported that street gangs were present at their school also nearly doubled, increasing from 15 percent in 1989 to 28 percent in 1995. During the 1996–1997 school year, 21 percent of all public high schools and 19 percent of all public middle schools reported to law enforcement agencies at least one serious violent crime such as murder, rape, sexual battery, physical attack, or fight with a weapon, robbery, or suicide (National Center for Educational Statistics, 1998).

ANGER AND THE LEARNING ENVIRONMENT

At the most fundamental level, *anger and violence undermine the learning environment.* This may seem obvious, but the importance of this fact cannot be overstated. Students cannot learn without first feeling safe and secure.

Safety must address the physical protection of students but should not ignore psychological security. The rash of school shootings has destroyed the sense of safety that used to permeate schools. School used to represent a safe haven for students. It was the place where over-burdened nine-year-olds could forget about adult responsibilities like caring for younger siblings or how the family would pay the rent. At school, students could be temporarily protected from the outside world. This sense of security is gone now, probably forever.

Children and adolescents know that violence can happen anywhere. Any teachers foolish enough to tell kids "A shooting can't happen here" immediately lose credibility with their students. They also misrepresent the truth and become just another adult that kids feel they can't trust.

Optimal learning takes place in an atmosphere of emotional safety. Will students openly discuss topics if they are concerned someone will become angry at them for expressing their opinions? The concern that their ideas will provoke hostility and criticism will discourage many students and make them less likely to participate. This robs their class-mates because it keeps their insights out of the learning environment. A teacher may never know what great thoughts students have if kids don't feel secure enough to offer their ideas in class.

Anger can also interfere with relationships between teachers and students. Children and adolescents generally seem to be less respectful and increasingly defiant toward authority figures. Some students' open displays of hostility make it difficult to form positive relationships with them. It is difficult for teachers to have a nurturing relationship with an adolescent who has just cursed at them. A solid teacher-student relationship is characterized by mutual respect.

A hostile and angry learning environment will also interfere with measurable outcomes such as student performance on standardized tests. The fact that anxiety affects achievement is beyond question.

There is a very clear negative correlation between anxiety and academic achievement. The higher the anxiety, which is affected by the level of observable and unobservable hostility, the lower the level of achievement. Increased hostility leads to lower achievement.

THE RELATIONSHIP BETWEEN ANGER
AND VIOLENCE

A considerable amount of evidence and the experience of clinicians everywhere support the contention that anger often precipitates violence (Rule and Nesdale, 1976). That is not to say there is a causal association between anger and violence; many students become angry without becoming aggressive. However, anger is often the trigger leading to violence. Perhaps Averill (1993) said it best when he stated that "anger can be thought of as an architect's blueprint. The availability of the blueprint does not cause a building to be constructed, but it does make the construction easier. In fact, without the blueprint, there might not be any construction at all" (p. 188).

Most students do not assault their classmates indiscriminately. It is possible for extremely disturbed students to behave aggressively without warning, but such occurrences are relatively infrequent. A small number of pupils are psychopathic and will act violently just for the sake of being aggressive, but this is the exception and not the rule. Most violence occurs because at least one, if not both, of the participants are enraged.

If there is any doubt that violence is the direct result of anger, try conducting this personal experiment. Think of the last time you were in a shouting match, kicked the family pet, or acted aggressively in some other manner. What predominant emotion were you experiencing at that moment? I'm willing to bet you were angry.

Some may argue that anger does not cause violence but rather that by acting violently a person *becomes* angry. The error in this logic can be demonstrated by considering football, one of the most violent yet socially acceptable activities in our culture. The goal of football is not physical violence in and of itself, but to play the game well a player must be aggressive. When a player makes a "great hit" and causes another player to momentarily take leave of his senses, there is no anger. In fact, the player who struck his opponent is usually elated to have made such a devastating tackle. Not only are the players not angry, they usually help each other up and pat each other on the back! There is usually no ill will. The players expect each other to act aggressively because that's the way the game is played.

Parents of children with anger difficulties can verify that anger is the cause of most serious problems at home and school. Teachers will support this contention, too. Stop by the office, time-out room, or wherever students are sent when they act inappropriately. Ask the students why they are being disciplined. A majority will be in the office because of some type of physical or verbal aggression.

Students are also disciplined for their unwillingness to comply with teacher demands, which is often a demonstration of passive aggression. Ask these children what they were feeling when they were acting up or refusing to comply with school rules, and most will tell you they were angry.

Some argue that anger is beneficial because it allows individuals to stand up for themselves. Undoubtedly, angry individuals are able to stand up for themselves, but nonangry, assertive individuals can achieve equally satisfactory results. Calm but assertive individuals rarely lose control while confronting someone. How many times has a nasty argument ensued from an innocent disagreement once individuals become angry? How many times, in the heat of the moment, do individuals say hurtful things that will never be forgiven or forgotten? Henry Ward Beecher advised, "Never forget what a man says to you when he is angry" (Peters, 1977).

GOALS OF THIS BOOK

The ideas set forth in this book are designed to bring about changes in various "roadblocks to learning." It is my firm belief that the programs and techniques discussed herein will help educators provide an atmosphere that is more conducive to growth, enrichment, and achievement. My intention is to provide readers with information that will aid in the acquisition of skills and the development of programs that will help children manage their behavior without resorting to violence. One of the keys to achieving this goal lies in teaching children to control their anger.

Numerous programs focus on teaching children how to express their anger in socially acceptable ways. These projects are often designed to teach children how to "get their anger out." Although there may be benefits from such programs for some students, that is not the goal or intention of this book. *The primary goal is to teach students how not to become angry in the first place.*

Many children and adolescents will insist that they should get their anger out even if it is only symbolically by hitting a pillow. Students will question the idea that they have a choice whether or not to *make themselves angry.* Quite simply, many will not believe that it is possible to deal with frustration and not become angry. They still want to "blow off steam" because they mistakenly believe that it's healthy to "express their anger."

It is important to acknowledge that suppressed anger is related to a number of medical conditions such as hypertension, coronary artery disease, and cancer (Greer and Morris, 1975; Harburg et al., 1991; Harburg, Blakelock, and Roeper, 1979, Spielberger et al., 1991). However, don't *assume* that suppressed anger is more damaging than expressed anger. That is not necessarily the case. In truth, the body knows no difference between repressed anger (anger held in) and expressed anger (anger let out). The changes in pulse, stomach acid secretion, and blood pressure are virtually identical. The feelings of anger (whether held in or let out) still cause physiological damage. There is additional information on this topic in chapter 2.

Anger is not an emotion most people would choose to experience if they knew they had a choice. It is an emotion of tension and desperation. Anger often occurs when people feel threatened and frustrated.

I am not saying that children and adolescents do not have the right to be angry. They have the right to feel any emotion, no matter what that feeling might be. People have the right to be angry and always will have that right. But students also have the right to know that there are many negative effects, both physical and emotional, of anger. They also have the right to learn how to control their anger and find themselves happier, healthier, and in fewer difficulties as a result of these changes in their lives.

Anger can be directly linked to violence, health problems, and interpersonal difficulties. It only makes sense to teach children how to control anger. Since habits are hard to break, it is also logical to provide children and adolescents with control techniques before patterns become firmly ingrained.

The philosophies and exercises examined in this book can be used with children as well as adolescents. Some people believe that this approach can only be applied to middle and high school students, but elementary students can understand and use these techniques. These ideas are introduced to all fourth-grade students in one district where I worked, but occasionally I have used these techniques with children in the second and third grades. The concepts remain the same, but the method of presentation must be adapted to be appropriate for their level of development. The approach is based on a philosophy known as Rational-Emotive Behavior Therapy (REBT), which is examined throughout this book.

CONCLUSION

Violence in our schools is a major problem. Anger often precipitates violence and is detrimental to classroom atmosphere and education in general. Students who are concerned about their safety and security will be unable to focus on learning.

Anger, whether held in or expressed, has many damaging effects on health. Helping students learn how *not* to become angry will either directly or indirectly benefit all those who are involved in the education of our children and adolescents.

CHAPTER 2

Hostility and Health: The Relationship between Anger, Stress, and Illness

Anger and hostility not only cause social and emotional problems but also have many damaging effects on an individual's physical health. There have been some interesting studies supporting the contention that anger leads to health difficulties.

Researchers have consistently found suppressed anger to be related to a number of medical conditions such as hypertension, coronary artery disease, and cancer (Greer and Morris, 1975; Harburg et al., 1991; Harburg, Blakelock, and Roeper, 1979; Spielberger et al., 1991). As mentioned in chapter 1, readers are cautioned not to assume that these findings suggest that "expressed anger" is healthier than "suppressed anger." Berkowitz (1970) has found that individuals who punish, curse at, or otherwise express aggression against others almost always begin to feel *more* angry instead of feeling less irate. Murray (1985) reports that when people are criticized, giving them an opportunity to express their anger makes them angrier. In a study by Mallik and McCandless (1966), third-graders were frustrated and irritated by a classmate (who was helping the researchers with the experiment). The children were given three choices for possible responses: 1) some were permitted to "talk it out" with adults, 2) some were allowed to play with guns to "get even" with the child who was annoying them, and 3) some were given an explanation by an adult of the child's annoying behavior (e.g., "He's tired," "He doesn't feel well today"). The researchers were somewhat surprised by the results. Talking it out with an adult did nothing to help diminish their anger. Playing with guns made the children *more* hostile and aggressive. Understanding why their classmate had acted that way was the most successful way to manage their anger.

Shekelle et al. (1983) conducted a study using 1,800 Western Electric workers, who were given a test to measure feelings of hostility. The participants were first asked to complete the hostility questionnaire in the late 1950s and subsequently tracked to determine if higher scores in hostility would correlate with health problems. The workers who were more hostile were 1.5 times more likely to develop coronary artery disease. These same workers had a higher rate of cancer, but the differences between the high and low hostility groups were not statistically significant.

Barefoot et al. have conducted a number of studies analyzing levels of hostility as a predictor of cardiovascular disease and death. Barefoot, Dahlstrom, and Williams (1983) followed 255 medical students at the University of North Carolina in the late 1950s and found that doctors who scored at or above the fifty-first percentile on the Hostility subscale on the Minnesota Multiphasic Personality Inventory (MMPI) were four to five times more likely to develop coronary artery disease. The authors of this project noted that *the hostile group was nearly seven times as likely to be deceased.*

Barefoot et al. (1989) followed 118 law students in the 1950s. Of the lawyers whose scores were in the upper quartile on a measure of hostility, nearly 20 percent were dead by age fifty. Only 4 percent of the lawyers who scored in the bottom quartile were dead.

A study examining hostility and cardiovascular disease symptoms was recently conducted by Iribarren et al. (2000). The subjects were 374 African American and Caucasian men and women. These individuals were studied over a ten-year period to assess the relationship between hostility (using the Cook-Medley Hostility scale) and coronary artery calcification. Subjects who obtained a hostility score of less than 14 (8 percent) were positive for arterial calcification. For hostility scores between 14 and 19, blockage increased to 9 percent for the group. With scores between 20 and 25, blockage levels involved 17 percent of the group. Finally, for hostility scores above 25, blockage was indicated in 18 percent of the group.

There is solid evidence that anger and stress actually weaken the body's immune system and make it more difficult to fight off diseases.

Siegel and Brown (1988) conducted surveys of 364 adolescent girls (grades seven through eleven). Testing was conducted in September ($r1$) and the following May ($r2$). Correlations between negative life events and illnesses were significant for both time periods ($r1 = .26$ and $r2 = .32$).

Researchers at Ohio State University have conducted research on changes in cellular immunity related to anger. The subjects used in this study were newlyweds who were asked to check into the OSU Clinical Research Center to control their diet, caffeine intake, and physical activity. The newlyweds were asked to resolve marital issues while they were videotaped. Researchers then coded their communications as high or low anger. Blood samples were taken prior to, during, and after the discussion of marital issues. The blood samples from couples coded as "high anger" demonstrated decreased levels of hormones designed to initiate immune activity and fighting bacteria (Kiecolt-Glaser et al., 1993).

Anger has also been associated with cholesterol levels. Using twenty-nine healthy Caucasian men as subjects, Waldstein et al. (1990) administered Spielberger's (1988) State-Trait Anger Expression Inventory and found statistically significant correlations between cholesterol level and trait anger ($r = .44$) and between cholesterol level and anger-out ($r = .46$). Similarly, Johnson et al. (1992) obtained lipid data on thirty-eight African American males and discovered significant correlations between trait anger and the LDL-HDL ratio.

CONCLUSION

Researchers have consistently found suppressed anger to be related to a number of medical conditions such as hypertension, coronary artery disease, and cancer. Expressed anger typically causes individuals to feel *more* angry instead of feeling less irate. There is solid evidence that anger and stress actually weaken the body's immune system and make it more difficult to fight off diseases.

CHAPTER 3

Characteristics of Angry and Aggressive Students

Anger is a normal human emotion and, in and of itself, there is nothing inherently wrong with anger. Everyone gets angry from time to time. It's what individuals *do* with their anger that is important. Does anger move them in a positive or negative direction? All too often, anger can lead to great difficulties for children and adolescents. This chapter examines the characteristics of angry and aggressive students.

THINKING PATTERNS IN ANGER-PRONE INDIVIDUALS

Deffenbacher (1993) has proposed that angry individuals tend to possess numerous cognitive processing patterns that lead to increased levels of anger. Following is a synopsis of Deffenbacher's beliefs about the type of cognitive errors often committed by anger-prone individuals.

1. *Poor estimation of probabilities*—overestimating the probability of negative outcomes and underestimating the likelihood of positive outcomes.
2. *Attributional errors*—believing negative acts are done intentionally with the express purpose of maliciously attacking one. Anger-prone individuals believe they have the ability to read others' minds.
3. *Overgeneralizations*—using overly broad terms when describing time (e.g., excessive use of "always" and "never") and using global descriptions for people (e.g., stupid, lazy).

4. *Dichotomous thinking*—employing black-and-white thinking.
5. *Inflammatory labeling*—using descriptive terms that are emotionally charged, which only increases the person's anger.
6. *Demandingness*—believing others *should* not act in certain ways or that they *must* not behave as they have, in fact, behaved.
7. *Catastrophic thinking*—evaluating unmet demands in an exaggeratedly negative fashion (e.g., "It's horrible, terrible, and awful things haven't gone my way.")

ANGER AND AT-RISK STUDENTS

High levels of anger in youth have been linked to increased risk for substance abuse, juvenile delinquency, interpersonal difficulties, and vocational and school-related problems (Deffenbacher et al. 1996; Liebsohn, Oetting, and Deffenbacher, 1994). Children who manifest high levels of anger at school are also at risk for a number of behavioral, social, and physical concerns and have poorer academic performance (Smith and Furlong, 1994; Smith et al., 1998).

Fryxell (2000) examined characteristics of fifth- and sixth-grade students who were designated as either high-anger or low-anger depending on teacher ratings and their scores on the Multidimensional School Anger Inventory (MSAI). Students designated as high-anger scored lower on a self-report measure of physical appearance and global self-worth. There were no racial differences in the composition of the high and low-anger groups. However, 83 percent of students in the high-anger group were male, whereas boys constituted only 33 percent of the low-anger group.

The family domain for the high-anger group was characterized by a lack of parental support. There was no relationship between parents' marital status and the degree of school anger reported by their children. High-anger group members were found to have significantly fewer friends and were more likely to have been teased by others both within and outside school. Appearance was the most often cited reason for being teased for both groups.

In another study related to family environment and anger, Lopez and Thurman (1993) reported that college students reporting high levels of anger on the Trait Anger Scale (TAS) (Spielberger et al., 1983) reported more family conflict. Scores on the TAS were negatively correlated with measures of organization, moral-religious emphasis, and intellectual-cultural orientation.

Other studies have examined the effect adults have on anger expression in children. Preschoolers report feeling stressed during anger interactions and may respond to adults' angry interactions by incorporating negative coping behaviors into their socializations with other children (Cummings, 1987). Covell and Abramovitch (1987) found that children commonly identify themselves or other family members as the causes of their mother's anger. Fifty-eight percent of the sample of 123 five- to fifteen-year-olds reported that their anger was precipitated by their families.

THE DEVELOPMENT OF AGGRESSIVE PATTERNS

An essential component of school violence prevention is understanding the development of aggressive behavior patterns. What does the existing research tell us about children who act violently? Are certain children prone to becoming aggressive?

Kenneth Dodge and his colleagues (Dodge, 1986; Dodge and Frame, 1982) theorize that children prone to aggressive behavior may have difficulties with social information processing (SIP). The SIP model can perhaps be understood by examining the similarities and differences between the human brain and a computer. In a computer, data are placed into the system and stored, to be retrieved at a later date. In people, information takes the shape of experiences in the world. Students each have a social history and a set of experiences that have affected them since birth. SIP postulates a dynamic human system, with each new experience having an impact on the child. Of course, human beings are infinitely more complex than computers, and this analogy runs the risk of oversimplifying the process of social interactions. This model focuses on the verbal learning process and memory as they affect social interactions.

Crick and Dodge (1994) have identified six steps or cognitive functions that children must master for effective social interactions: encoding, representation/interpretation, goal selection, response access, response decision, and behavioral enactment.

Encoding

The first step involves children attending to events in their immediate environment. Each social event comprises a tremendous variety of information. Also, each interaction contains a lot of "data." Humans have a wide array of cues to select from during a social interaction. Does the child focus on the verbal message? If so, what portion of the message, the tone of voice, the language? Or does the child focus on visual input such as the speaker's smile? Children must be able to attend to relevant cues.

Aggressive children have a strong tendency to attend to hostile cues, whereas their classmates attend to nonhostile cues. For example, while she was passing back papers, Marcia dropped Steve's worksheet after bumping into his desk. She immediately smiled, said "Sorry," and picked up his paper, placing it on his desk. Steve's attention was drawn to Marcia's bumping into his desk and dropping his paper, and he ignored her smile, apology, and successful recovery of his paper.

Dodge has also studied cue utilization during the encoding stage (Dodge, 1986). That is, of all the social cues available during an interaction, which cues are attended to and which are ignored? Students prone to aggression tend to make more hostile attributions ("She tried to bump into me") than do nonaggressive classmates.

Representation/Interpretation

Once students have selected a cue out of all the information available during a social interaction, they must interpret the cue by matching the event with an occurrence stored in their memory. This phase is similar to a computer performing a "search" task. Of all the possible files in storage, the computer tries to find the closest match. Of course, a computer is operating without the interference of emotional baggage. Dodge (1986) reported that many aggressive students have a tendency to make a hostile attribution. ("She tried to bump into me because she was trying to hurt me.")

It is impossible to say with certainty what effect prior experiences have on these findings, but it may be considerable. Recall Cummings's (1987) finding that children respond to adults' angry interactions by incorporating negative coping behaviors into their socializations with other children. Research also indicates that students exposed to violence are more likely to engage in violent acts, often as preemptive strikes in the face of perceived threats (Singer et al., 1984).

Goal Selection

Once the event has been interpreted, the child will establish some type of emotional or behavioral goal for the social interaction. Goals can be influenced by

1. emotional states, such as anger;
2. temperament issues;
3. media influences; and
4. cultural or peer group norms (in this case, norms for a fifth-grade male).

Steve would most likely choose a retaliatory goal due to his interpretation that Marcia's behavior was intentional and hostile toward him.

Response Access

To be able to make a response, children first need to generate a mental representation of possible choices. Any number of possible responses could be mentally constructed and tested by Steve. Dodge and Frame (1982) found that children who have a history of aggressive behavior are not able to generate as many potential solutions as nonaggressive students can. Steve will be limited in the options he can summon as he tries to decide how to deal with Marcia.

Response Decision

The fifth step is the point at which the child chooses his or her response from the possible alternatives summoned up during the response access phase. In short, it is decision-making time.

It should not be surprising that aggressive children appear to have a bias toward favoring aggressive responses. They do not evaluate non-aggressive responses as thoroughly.

Behavioral Enactment

Children enact the behavioral response they have selected. To be successful they must have the skills required to complete the selected action.

For example, Steve may have selected the option of writing Marcia a note and asking if she was really sorry for bumping his desk and dropping his paper. For his selection to be successful, he will have to have the writing skills to form a question so as not to sound accusatory. There is a significant difference between, "Why did you bump into my desk like that?" and "Why did you bump into my desk? You weren't trying to hurt me, were you?" Steve may not have the linguistic sophistication to make his query sound like a question and not an accusation.

What makes this process so difficult for some children is that the entire interaction between Steve and Marcia took place in less than two seconds. Each behavioral output from either Steve or Marcia starts a new social interaction, with the information learned from the bump of a desk now being employed to guide decision making in the future. Students don't have the luxury of spending time to understand what is occurring in their lives.

THE NEUROLOGY OF ANGER

Emotions are largely the result of activity deep within the brain in an area known as the limbic system. Higher-level abilities such as reasoning and abstract thought are controlled by the frontal lobes.

When individuals become enraged the limbic system "overrides" the reasoning abilities of the frontal lobes. Rational thought is very difficult, if not impossible, during episodes of anger. Neurologically, it makes perfect sense that individuals say and do foolish things when they are angry. That's how humans are "wired." It is no coincidence that the word "mad" has two meanings: angry and crazy.

NEUROLOGICAL IMPAIRMENT AND AGGRESSION

Researchers such as Soloman and Kleeman (1971) have theorized that violence, when unprovoked or associated with impaired consciousness and confusion, may have neurological origins. They speculate that some unspecified disease of the limbic system or frontal lobes may be the cause of the aggression.

Evidence of neurological abnormality in violence-prone individuals dates back to 1951 (Gibbs and Gibbs). Other evidence of neurological impairment as a factor in violent behavior comes from a study by Murdoch (1972) in which aggressive psychopaths were found to have more cerebral instability in brain wave patterns than nonviolent prisoners did. Williams (1969) also found that aggressive criminals produced significantly more abnormal brain wave activity than did otherwise "normal" criminals.

Dorothy Otnow Lewis (1981) conducted a fascinating series of studies on this topic. Initially Lewis compared delinquents and nondelinquents and found that the former had significantly more hospital visits, accidents, and injuries than the latter. Next she compared imprisoned delinquents with nonimprisoned delinquents. Lewis used the factor of incarceration as a means of taking into consideration the seriousness of the crime. With respect to the boys in prison, 62.3 percent had suffered from serious face or head injuries, compared to 44.6 percent of the nonimprisoned subjects. Nearly one-third of the imprisoned boys had been injured severely enough to warrant skull X rays, compared to only 13.1 percent of the less violent delinquents.

Lewis next compared two groups, a sample of incarcerated delinquent boys who had committed serious crimes such as murder or rape and a sample of less violent boys who had committed crimes such as physically fighting and threatening others with weapons. The boys who had committed the severely violent crimes exhibited a higher incidence of symptoms associated with temporal lobe epilepsy (such as blackouts) and paranoid thinking than did the other group of subjects. Almost 30 percent of the violent delinquents had grossly abnormal EEGs or epilepsy or both, whereas none of the other delinquents had either sign.

STABILITY OF BEHAVIOR PATTERNS

There has been a great deal written about resiliency and reclaiming at-risk youth. Adults have a strong desire to believe that all children can be "saved." Teachers and other school professionals have to have hope. Without hope of eventual change, why intervene? Why make an attempt to help kids if the effort is doomed to fail?

Unfortunately, aggression in children is fairly stable. Teacher-rated aggression at age eight predicted self-reported aggression ten years later at age eighteen (Farrington, 1977). When eight-year-olds were asked to rate their peers in terms of aggressiveness, those ratings predicted self-reports of aggression twenty-two years later at age thirty (Eron et al., 1987).

CHARACTERISTICS OF SCHOOL SHOOTERS

Following the rash of school shootings in the late 1990s, the FBI compiled a team of behavioral specialists to analyze the characteristics of school shooters. The following sections review the report, *The School Shooter: A Threat Perspective Assessment* (1999), focusing on personality traits and behaviors of school shooters.

Leakage

"Leakage" occurs when a student intentionally or unintentionally reveals clues to feelings, thoughts, fantasies, or intentions that may signal an impending violent act. These clues can take the form of subtle threats, boasts, innuendoes, predictions, or ultimatums. They may be spoken or conveyed in stories, diary entries, essays, poems, letters, songs, drawings, doodles, tattoos, or videos (as was the case with Dylan Kleibold and Eric Harris).

The FBI noted, "Leakage can be a cry for help, a sign of inner conflict, or boasts that may look empty but actually express a serious threat. Leakage is considered to be one of the most important clues that may precede an adolescent's violent act."

Anger Management Problems

Rather than expressing anger in appropriate ways, the student consistently tends to have temper tantrums or to brood in sulky, seething silence. His or her anger may come in unpredictable and uncontrollable outbursts and may be accompanied by expressions of unfounded prejudice, dislike, or even hatred toward individuals or groups.

Most, if not all, of the school shooters were very angry young men. Some displayed their anger for the world to see while others secretly seethed, keeping their anger buried.

Low Tolerance for Frustration

The student is easily insulted, angered, and hurt by real or perceived injustices done to him or her by others and has great difficulty tolerating frustration.

Poor Coping Skills

The student consistently shows little, if any, ability to deal with frustration, criticism, disappointment, failure, rejection, or humiliation. His or her response is typically inappropriate, exaggerated, or disproportionate.

Lack of Resiliency

The student lacks resiliency and has a difficult time bouncing back from a frustrating or disappointing experience.

Failed Love Relationship

The student may feel rejected or humiliated after the end of a love relationship and cannot accept or come to terms with the rejection. This was true in several of the school shootings in 1998. Mitchell Johnson, thirteen at the time of the shooting in Jonesboro, Arkansas, was angry with several of the girls in his class, apparently because they had broken up with him.

"Injustice Collector"

The student harbors resentment over real or perceived injustices. No matter how much time has passed, the "injustice collector" will not forget or forgive those wrongs or the people he or she believes are responsible. Several shooters kept hit lists of the names of people they felt had wronged them.

Depression

The student shows features of depression such as lethargy, physical fatigue, a morose or dark outlook on life, a sense of malaise, and loss of interest in activities that he or she once enjoyed.

Adolescents may show different signs than those normally associated with depression. Some depressed adolescents may display unpredictable and uncontrolled outbursts of anger, a generalized and excessive hatred toward everyone else, and feelings of hopelessness about the future. Other behaviors include psychomotor agitation, restlessness, inattention, sleep and eating disorders, and a markedly diminished interest in almost all activities that previously occupied and interested them.

The connection between anger and depression is examined in greater detail in chapter 8. The work of Aaron Beck (Beck and Shaw, 1977) is incorporated to provide not only an etiological examination but a treatment model as well.

Fascination with Violence-Filled Entertainment

The student demonstrates an unusual fascination with movies, TV shows, computer games, music videos, or printed material focusing intensively on themes of violence, hatred, control, power, death, and destruction. He or she may incessantly watch one movie or read and reread one book with violent content, perhaps involving school violence. Themes of hatred, violence, weapons, and mass destruction recur in virtually all of the student's activities, hobbies, and pastimes.

The student spends inordinate amounts of time playing video games with violent themes and seems more interested in the violent images than in the game itself. On the Internet, the student regularly searches for web sites involving violence, weapons, and other disturbing subjects.

Narcissism That Masks Low Self-Esteem

The student is self-centered, lacks insight into others' feelings, and blames others for his or her own failures. The narcissistic student may embrace the role of a victim to elicit sympathy and to feel temporarily superior to others. He or she displays signs of paranoia and assumes an attitude of self-importance or grandiosity that masks feelings of unworthiness. A narcissistic student may be either very thin-skinned or very thick-skinned in responding to criticism. Although he or she may display an arrogant attitude, the student's conduct often appears to veil an underlying low self-esteem. He or she avoids high visibility or involvement in school activities.

Alienation

The student consistently behaves as though he or she feels different or estranged from others. This sense of separateness is more than just being a loner. It can involve feelings of isolation, sadness, and loneliness.

Dehumanizing Others

The student consistently fails to see others as fellow humans. He or she characteristically views other people as "nonpersons" or objects.

Lack of Empathy

The student shows an inability to understand the feelings of others and appears unconcerned about anyone else's feelings (see "Narcissism" above).

Exaggerated Sense of Entitlement

The student constantly expects special treatment and has a tendency to react negatively if he or she doesn't get the treatment he or she feels entitled to.

High Need for Attention

The student shows an exaggerated need for attention, whether positive or negative.

Externalizing Blame

The student consistently refuses to take responsibility for his or her own actions and typically faults other people, events, or situations for any failings or shortcomings.

These are the students who refuse to accept the premise that events do not make them angry. They cannot admit that their thoughts, beliefs, and attitudes *about* events make them angry. To take ownership of their feelings is frightening for these students because it places them in a position of taking responsibility for their feelings and behavior.

Intolerance

The student often expresses racial prejudice or intolerant attitudes toward minorities or displays slogans or symbols of intolerance in the form of such things as tattoos, jewelry, clothing, bumper stickers, and book covers.

Seeking to Manipulate Others Due to a Lack of Trust

The student consistently attempts to con and manipulate others and win their trust while at the same time being untrusting and chronically suspicious of others' motives and intentions. This lack of trust may approach a clinically paranoid state. The student may express the belief that society has no trustworthy institution or mechanism for achieving justice or resolving conflict, and that if something bothers him or her, he or she has to settle it in his or her own way.

Closed Social Group

The student appears introverted, with acquaintances rather than friends, or associates only with a single small group that seems to exclude everyone else. Students who threaten or carry out violent acts are not necessarily loners. The student often has a peer group, and the composition and qualities of peer groups can be important pieces of information in assessing the danger that a threat will be acted on.

Change in Behavior

The student's behavior changes dramatically. His or her academic performance may decline, or he or she may show a reckless disregard for school rules, schedules, dress codes, and other regulations.

Being Rigid and Opinionated

The student appears rigid, judgmental, and cynical, and voices strong opinions on subjects about which he or she has little knowledge. He or she disregards facts, logic, and reasoning that might challenge these opinions. Again, rational explanations are quickly discounted by the school shooter. The attitude, "It is true because I believe it to be true," is common.

Unusual Interest in Sensational Violence

The student demonstrates an unusual interest in school shootings and other heavily publicized acts of violence. He or she may declare admiration for those who committed the acts and may explicitly express a desire to carry out a similar act in his or her own school, possibly as an act of "justice."

Readers who interact with adolescents on a daily basis will realize that this list could include a significant percentage of high school students. Also keep in mind that none of the shooters shows *all* these characteristics. Descriptors of school shooters provide very few practical benefits to practitioners as to which students might actually act on violent impulses. However, these descriptions do provide valuable information regarding which students might need close monitoring and intervention.

CONCLUSION

Anger-prone individuals tend to possess numerous cognitive processing patterns that lead to increased levels of anger. They are also at risk for a number of behavioral, social, and physical concerns. High levels of anger and hostility are related to poorer academic performance.

Kenneth Dodge and his colleagues have developed a useful model (SIP) for explaining the development of aggressive behavior patterns. Other researchers have found patterns of neurological dysfunction in aggressive youths, who statistically are more likely to have suffered some type of significant head injury. The FBI profile of school shooters points out a host of factors such as leakage, low frustration tolerance, anger management difficulties, narcissism, and alienation.

CHAPTER 4

Two Opposing Theories on the Cause of Anger in Children and Adolescents

Most individuals (including children and adolescents) believe that other *people* and *things* make them angry. Hardly a day passes without hearing remarks that support this contention:

"He made me so angry."
"She told me 'no' and that really ticked me off."
"When people say things behind my back, it makes me so mad."

One theory regarding the source of anger states that anger is an emotion caused by frustration (Dollard et al., 1939). This belief, which is known as the *frustration-aggression hypothesis,* states that all aggression is caused by negative emotional arousal, typically arising from frustrating experiences that block an individual from achieving his or her goal. This arousal, according to the theory, can only be reduced by acting aggressively.

Consider the example of Billy, a twelve-year-old fifth-grade student. His teacher, Mr. Lucht, tells Billy that in order to go on the field trip he must not receive any detention the week of the trip. On the day prior to the long-awaited trip, Billy breaks several rules during music class and receives detention from Mr. Buehner, the music teacher. Billy apologizes and promises to behave more appropriately in the future. Mr. Buehner accepts Billy's apology but informs Billy that he will still have to serve the detention he received in music class.

News also gets back to Mr. Lucht that Billy received detention. He informs Billy, as per their agreement, that he will be unable to go on the field trip. Billy becomes enraged and screams, "It's not fair! Other

kids were talking in music and they didn't get detention. You and Buehner are out to get me." The question is, what is causing Billy's anger?

According to the frustration-aggression hypothesis, his anger is due
to the fact that he is being blocked from his goal (i.e., going on the field
trip). Had Billy not received detention he would not be angry, so the
cause of his anger is detention.

There is a theory that would suggest another source for Billy's
anger—namely, Billy. According to Rational-Emotive Behavior Therapy (REBT), his anger is not being caused by detention or his frustration but by his demand that he not be frustrated. In other words, it's not
detention that is causing his anger, it is his *demand* about detention
(i.e., "It's not fair and I have to be treated fairly." "I really want to go
on the field trip and I should have what I really want.") Which theory
is correct?

If the frustration-aggression hypothesis is correct, every time children and adolescents are frustrated they will become angry because
frustration *causes* anger. The question then becomes, "Could other
children have the same experience (i.e., receive detention and miss the
field trip) and *not* get angry?" This is entirely possible because students often react differently to the same situation.

Billy could have received detention, missed the field trip, and not
have been angry or at least only have been moderately irritated. Instead
of thinking and stating, "It's not fair! Other kids were talking in music
class and they didn't get detention," Billy could have thought, "I knew
the rule Mr. Buehner has about talking without raising your hand first.
The punishment is fair and even though I don't like it, I accept it." By
accepting responsibility for his behavior, Billy could acknowledge that
he had acted inappropriately and deserved detention.

It is even possible for Billy to believe he had been treated unfairly
but still refuse to make himself angry. He could believe, "It's not fair.
I really don't deserve this punishment. Mr. Buehner made a mistake
but I guess we all do that from time to time. I'd like it if I was being
treated fairly but I guess I don't always get what I want."

He would still be disappointed about missing the field trip but would
not be enraged. The rational thought, "It's not fair but people have the
right to make mistakes" would keep his emotional response at an
appropriate level.

Ellis (1973) draws a distinction between healthy and unhealthy anger. *Healthy anger* is moderate in its intensity and includes such feelings as *irritation, disappointment,* and *displeasure.* Such emotions are viewed as healthy because they motivate people to change. By feeling irritated about missing the field trip, students will try to act more appropriately so they will be able to attend future events. Irritation or disappointment will do nothing to interfere with their behaving in a manner that will allow them to be included in the next field trip. Also, their irritation will serve as a reminder to follow the class rules.

Emotions such as *anger, rage, hate,* and *bitterness* are deemed *unhealthy* because they do little to aid in survival and help people reach their goals. If Billy's goal is to attend the next field trip, rage and hatred directed toward his teachers will probably interfere with his ability to act in an appropriate manner. Such emotions will certainly not help him control his behavior.

The Russian neuropsychologist Luria (1973) stated that extreme anger precludes higher-level reasoning from mediating behavior due to the arousal of the limbic system. When the limbic system is aroused, people tend to react without first considering the consequences of their actions.

APPROPRIATE EMOTIONAL INTENSITY FOR A SITUATION

How do we tell the difference between healthy and unhealthy anger? This is important because it would be unhealthy, not to mention impossible, to eliminate anger from students' lives. As mentioned previously, healthy anger can be beneficial.

Anger that is healthy reaches an appropriate level of intensity for a given situation. This "healthy anger" keeps the response in line with the intensity of the event. In other words, rational anger does not use more feeling than is necessary to respond to the situation. It is necessary to determine if the intensity of the feeling was appropriate. This can usually be accomplished using the following procedure.

After a child has told you about an experience in which he made himself angry (for example, having been told he couldn't go on a field trip), ask the child, "If we asked 100 students your age how angry they would be if they were told they couldn't go on the field trip, what do you think the average would be? On our scale let's say '1' is not angry at all and '100' is very angry." The child will usually respond with a rating somewhere in the middle, perhaps 55. The next question is, "How angry did you make yourself?" The usual response is higher than the theoretical "average" of 100 students; in this example let's say 85. This difference (between 55 and 85) is a good way of showing the student he is using more emotion than necessary in this situation. By his own estimate of the average for the class, the student has just told you that the proper intensity would result in angry feelings of 55, and he rated the intensity of his feelings to be 30 points above that. The goal is to bring the student's emotional reaction down to an appropriate level that is in line with the situation.

It is also appropriate to explain that almost no one would *like* being told he or she would have to miss a field trip. Of course a student would be disappointed or irritated; that is perfectly understandable. The problem arises when a student *overreacts* and uses more intensity than the situation warrants.

Occasionally a student will say the average feelings of anger for 100 classmates would be 95. This poses a bit of a problem, but usually the student can be "talked down" with a small amount of effort by the counselor. By reasoning with the student that missing one field trip is not a complete and total catastrophe to most people, she can often be convinced to adjust the average score down to a lower number. The following example should help clarify how reasoning with the student will usually get her to lower the rating.

Therapist: Billy, you say that the average from your class if they found out they were missing the field trip would be 95.

Billy: At least that high. Field trips are great . . . lots better than being here in school.

T: Well, what if the teacher said that not only would students not get to go on the field trip but they would also have to do extra homework. How mad would they be?

B: 150!

T: Remember, we can only go to 100.

B: Then 100.

T: So missing the trip and extra homework would be the all time tops for anger, the maddest you could be?

B: Yeah.

T: Okay, what if not only did you miss the trip and get extra homework but the teacher said you had to stay in from recess next week and redo all the work from the week before. Where would you be on the scale now?

B: 250!

T: So you'd be even madder than just missing the trip and extra homework?

B: Sure . . . that wouldn't be fair.

T: Okay, now let's think back for minute to when we were pretending you would miss the field trip and get extra home work. Where would you be on the scale now? You said that was 100 a minute ago but where would it be now?

B: Maybe . . . 85.

T: So not as high now. Is that because you're saying you wouldn't be as mad if the teacher didn't make you redo the homework?

B: Yeah, because at least we wouldn't have to do a bunch of homework over again.

T: Okay, now let's get back to the situation that actually exists, missing the field trip. Where would you be on the scale now?

B: Probably about 70 or 75.

Sometimes students will not budge and insist that most people would rate their anger at 95 out of 100. When this happens it is time to conduct some on-the-spot "research." This is accomplished by walking into the hall and asking the first five to ten students you see the same question and recording their responses to find an actual average. I've done this numerous times, and it has never failed to produce a lower average than the 95 we are using in this example. Once you have this average you can proceed to the next question, "How angry did you make yourself?" Rest assured that this number will be quite high, especially if the student thinks everyone will have anger at 95 or above.

Simply using this activity can be eye opening to students once they realize that not everyone makes themselves enraged when they do not get what they want. Many children experience disappointment but do not overreact. Students who have anger problems often do not realize they have that option because they have been "exploding" for years.

Kids have a difficult time understanding that others who experience the same events can and do feel differently. Demonstrating that not everyone gets as upset as they do about certain situations gives anger-prone students the opportunity to reconsider their reactions to everyday events.

People often convince themselves and others that events cause them to be angry, but this can be disproved. This is not to say that an event (i.e., missing the movies) has no influence over the child's emotional reaction. Events definitely contribute to feelings but are not solely responsible for emotional reactions. Keep this distinction in mind, because it is important in helping children control their anger. *Events cannot be changed; thoughts and beliefs can.* The beliefs, attitudes, and ideas about events are primarily responsible for the emotional reactions people choose.

RATIONAL-EMOTIVE BEHAVIOR THERAPY:
A BRIEF OVERVIEW

In direct opposition to the frustration-aggression hypothesis is REBT. Its founder, Albert Ellis, was influenced by the stoic philosopher Epictetus, who stated, "Men are disturbed not by things, but by the views they take of them." In other words, *people feel how they think.*

As previously stated, it comes as a shock to most people to find out that others cannot *make* them angry. Most children and adolescents simply do not believe that being given detention, for example, did not make them upset. In reality, they upset themselves with their thoughts *about* being given detention.

To illustrate this point, let's take an example in which ten students are held in from recess. Would all ten react in the same manner? Probably not, because different students would respond with different emotions. Some would be angry, some indifferent, and some could even be happy. The individual emotional responses would be determined by the thoughts the students had concerning the event (i.e., being held in from recess). Once again, people feel how they think.

Students who made themselves angry would probably be thinking something such as, "I shouldn't have to miss recess. It's not fair and my teacher is a jerk for treating me unfairly." Indifference could be produced by the belief, "I don't mind missing recess. It's cold and rainy out today anyway." A student could even be happy if he or she believed, "Since I have to stay in from recess, I'll have time to finish my math homework."

If an event caused a specific emotion, it would be impossible for the same event to produce several different emotions. This supports the idea that events don't cause emotions. Beliefs *about* events determine emotional reactions.

Beliefs can either be *rational* or *irrational,* depending on several factors. A belief that promotes survival and happiness is generally considered to be rational. Walen, DiGiuseppe, and Wessler (1980) provided the following information as a guide to determine if a belief is rational or irrational:

Rational Beliefs
- are true
- can be supported by evidence or proof
- are logical
- are *not* absolute commands
- are desires, wishes, hopes, and preferences
- produce moderate emotions such as sadness, irritation, and concern
- help you reach your goals

Irrational Beliefs
- are false
- lead to inaccurate deductions
- often are overgeneralizations
- are commands, shoulds, and needs
- lead to disturbed emotions such as depression, rage, and anxiety
- hinder you from reaching your goals

Irrational beliefs often are produced by overgeneralizations. Ellis (1977b) stated that a *belief remains rational so long as it does not extend an evaluation of the action into an evaluation of the person.* It is best to keep this distinction in mind when working with students who have anger problems. It is not uncommon for students to have the irrational belief that because someone acted in a rotten manner, he or she is a rotten person. Many students (and teachers, counselors, parents, principals, etc.) do not understand that there are no rotten people, just people who at times act rottenly. Although this may seem like a matter of semantics, the distinction is important and is examined in chapter 7.

Maultsby (1975) encourages his clients to ask the following questions to determine if a belief is rational:

1. Can I prove this belief to be true?
2. Does this belief help to protect my life and health?
3. Does this belief help me get what I want?
4. Does this thinking help me to avoid unwanted conflicts with others?
5. Does this belief help me to feel the emotions I want to feel?

If the answer is "yes" to any three of these questions, the belief is mostly rational. If two or fewer are answered affirmatively, a belief is irrational and self-defeating.

THE ABCs OF REBT

Rational-Emotive Behavior Therapy uses the ABC system of problem identification, clarification, and resolution. This system is designed to help clients target irrational beliefs and replace them with rational alternatives. This model is helpful because it gives the therapist and client a common frame of reference from which to work. Many REBT counselors like to diagram the ABCs on paper or a blackboard. Adding this visual component is beneficial because it incorporates another modality to help in retrieval of the information.

In the ABC system, "A" stands for the *activating event* that occurs immediately before a client becomes upset. The "A" is "the happening" or "situation." A student could be upset because he or she was called a name or any number of other occurrences. Eating lunch, walking to school, riding a bike, and getting detention are all examples of an "activating event."

The "C" stands for the *consequence*. What feeling was the client experiencing, or what did he or she do? It is important to try to get clients to be as specific as possible when labeling their feelings. "I feel bad" isn't very helpful because the term "bad" could represent any number of emotions from anger to depression to guilt. It is also possible for clients to feel a combination of emotions at "C." It's possible for a child to simultaneously feel anxious and angry. In such a case, keep in mind that each emotion is caused by a distinctive thought.

People commonly believe that "A" causes "C" (e.g., being picked last for the softball team causes anger), but that is not correct. There is a middle part ("B") between "A" and "C" that actually causes the emotion.

"B" stands for *belief* or what an individual tells himself or herself about the activating event at point "A." When searching for the "B" try to get clients to focus on the thoughts they had *about the "A."* Many students will relay unrelated thoughts such as, "I'm a good softball player and I shouldn't be picked last." Encourage clients to focus on their beliefs about the "A" (e.g., "You may be a great softball player but getting picked last did not cause you to become angry and swear at the gym teacher. What were you saying to yourself about being picked last?").

It is recommended that counselors diagram the ABCs with nearly every client, especially early in treatment. Eventually clients can become proficient at performing their own ABC analysis, but it takes practice. Once the irrational belief at point "B" is clearly defined, it is time to move on to "D," which stands for *disputation.*

As the name implies, disputation is the point at which the counselor disputes or debates with clients about their irrational beliefs at point "B." There are numerous disputation techniques, which are discussed in chapter 7. In this chapter we focus on the basics of the ABC system.

The final step is "E," which stands for the new *effect* produced by substituting a rational belief for an irrational belief. The goal at point "E" may be just to have the client produce a moderate emotional response (such as irritation) rather than unhealthy anger or rage.

There is a big difference between irritation, which is an appropriate response, and rage, which will do nothing to help clients survive, reach their goals, or experience the emotions they want to experience.

THE PRIMARY BELIEF LEADING TO ANGER

Rational-Emotive Behavior Therapy postulates that the primary irrational belief causing anger is the idea that "Things *should* be the way I want them to be." Anger is almost always created by a *demand* of some type. Typically the demand is formulated using key words such as *should, must, ought to,* and *have to.*

Ellis (1962; 1976) has stated on numerous occasions that humans have a tendency to escalate their desires and wishes into absolute demands. This is especially true when these desires are strong. The fact that nearly all humans share this habit has led Ellis to believe that thinking irrationally is a basic biological tendency. Undoubtedly this tendency is also influenced by sociocultural factors. The fact remains that nearly all humans have the tendency to take a personal desire and turn it into a demand.

A child may view a commercial for a soon-to-be released movie and think, "I really want to see that movie." Is this a rational belief? Absolutely. The child is expressing a desire and there is evidence to support it. The fact that the child continually asks his parents to take him to see the movie is evidence that he does indeed want to see the film. The problem lies in the fact that there is typically a second portion to this statement that is also affecting how the child feels. This second portion is unspoken and usually occurs without the child's awareness. The second portion adds, "I really want to see that movie *and therefore I have to see it!*" This second portion is an absolute demand and is the reason the child is angry when his parents refuse to take him as soon as the movie comes to town. The second portion is irrational and normally takes place at a preconscious level below the child's awareness. The child will report only the thoughts that he is aware of at that time. Clients will tell you, "I'm not demanding anything," but trust the theory. *If there is anger, there is a demand.* If anger is present, be assured that a demand is also present, even if a child claims he or she isn't demanding anything. Where there's smoke, there's fire.

While the primary beliefs leading to anger are demands in one form or another, there are also secondary corollaries that contribute to anger. These beliefs are considered secondary because they tend to be focused on the nature of the offending party or the nature of the perceived misdeed. Ellis (1977b) stated that the following beliefs also lead to anger:

1. How *awful* for you to have treated me so unfairly!
2. I *can't stand* you treating me in such a manner!
3. Because you have acted in that manner toward me, I find you a *rotten person.*

The first corollary is irrational because the term "awful" is an immeasurable and indefinable term. When students use the term "awful" to describe an event they often think they mean "bad" or "very bad." Their actual emotional meaning associated with the term "awful" appears to mean worse than 100 percent bad. It is impossible for an event to be worse than 100 percent bad, because no matter how bad a particular event happened to be, it could always be worse. Even though it is impossible for something to be worse than 100 percent bad, it is possible to make an event seem worse by exaggerating its "badness."

After students agree that nothing can be worse than 100 percent bad, it can be helpful to have them describe the worst event they can imagine. Then challenge them to somehow make the event even worse. This is usually fairly easy. Most events they will offer are certainly not tragedies in the adult sense of the word. Students may say the worst event they can imagine is getting an "F" in science. This can easily become worse by getting "Fs" in all classes.

The second corollary, which states that an individual *"can't stand"* being treated in such a manner, is irrational because nothing is so bad that a person can't stand the event. This type of thinking is also an example of exaggerating an event's badness. If an unpleasant event is inevitable (such as death), believing that one can't stand the event will only create unnecessary anxiety and won't accomplish anything productive. It certainly won't assist the person in avoiding death.

With anger, clients might believe they cannot stand being treated unfairly when in reality they have been treated unfairly hundreds of times in the past and managed to stand it. To be unable to stand something literally means that if the event were to occur it would kill the individual. If it were true that people are unable to stand being treated unfairly, then everyone would have died at a very early age.

The third corollary ("I find you a rotten person!") makes the mistake of overgeneralizing from the evaluation of an act to the evaluation of the person committing the act. No matter how rotten someone acted, he or she is still not a rotten person. To state that a person is rotten would mean that every act the person has committed (or will commit) has been rotten, and that is impossible. To believe someone is "rotten" dehumanizes the person and makes it acceptable to aggress against that individual.

ANGER AS GRANDIOSITY

Freud (1963) and Adler (1968) both noted that nearly all anger stems from childish grandiosity. Ellis (1977a) stated that since the possibility exists that others *can* treat us well, people mistakenly believe that others *should* treat us well. If there is one phrase to remember from this entire book it is this: *All anger is grandiosity.*

Hauck (1980) makes the point that anger is produced by the grandiose belief that "my desires and wishes MUST be fulfilled." Such a belief is grandiose because it is presumes that one's personal preferences and wishes are more important than everyone else's. "Because I want something to be a certain way it *must* be that way" is about as grandiose as it gets!

When people are angry they are declaring commandments for the entire universe and then damning everyone who dares to disobey them. The problem with this type of thinking is that one individual does *not* run the universe. This can be pointed out to a student, as I demonstrate in the following short transcription from a session. The student and I were working together for a few weeks due to his problems with anger. He was referred to me because he kept finding himself in the principal's office for a variety of problems that ranged from fist fighting to defying teachers to swearing at other adults in the building. Before this session he was in the time-out room because he had spit on the bathroom floor.

Steve: I hate Mike. He told the teacher I spit on the floor in the bathroom.

Therapist: Did you spit on the floor?

S: Yes, but he shouldn't have told . . . the narc.

T: Let's write down what you just said. (Writes down "He shouldn't have told.") Is that a true belief?

S: Probably not.

T: Why isn't it?

S: I don't know but whenever you ask me if a belief is true, it almost never is.

T: Is that statement a wish or a demand?

S: A demand, I guess.

T: What's the problem with demanding Mike do what you want?

S: I guess it's because he doesn't have to.

T: That's right. Let me tell you a secret. *You don't run the universe.*

S: I know that.

T: But when you say things like, "He shouldn't have told," what you're sort of saying is, "I, Steve the almighty, commands that you not tell." That's like going outside and demanding that it not rain.

S: That's stupid.

T: That would be pretty stupid, wouldn't it? But you know what, you've got just as much control over the weather as you do over Mike. What are the only two things you can control in this entire world?

S: Myself and . . . I forget.

T: What you think and what you do.

PATIENCE AND LOW FRUSTRATION TOLERANCE

It seems that over the past few years, individuals have become less patient and tolerant than ever before. The truth is that people have never been all that patient and tolerant. Social scientists have been quick to blame things like television, with its ever-changing images, for being primarily responsible for this change in our nation's youth. Kids today expect everything to be immediately gratifying. Our culture has produced many time-saving devices that make tasks easier to complete. In the long run these conveniences, along with the other changes in our culture, have taken a toll on our children.

There appears to be an increase in the adoption of the irrational belief that "Things have to be easy." It is alarming how many children seem to believe, "My life should be completely free of hassles," which is a derivative of "Things have to be easy." Other common corollaries are:

"All things have to be enjoyable."

"Things have to go my way."

"If things aren't fun, it's horrible."

The effects of such thinking can be seen and felt on a cultural level. Activities that require patience and discipline are on the decline. If there is not an immediate payback, kids who hold these beliefs will not be interested.

This cultural phenomenon has undoubtedly influenced the declining academic skills of today's students. The performance of our nation's students will never increase without a change in these attitudes. The attitude that "everything should be fun" affects their work ethic. Not everything can be fun. Most things that are worth pursuing take an extended period of time to come to fruition.

This syndrome of immediate payback, little patience, and even less self-discipline can be categorized as *low frustration tolerance (LFT)*. The LFT syndrome, and the accompanying set of irrational ideas that produce it, permeates a child's thinking in all areas. It affects nearly every phase of the student's life, from academic, to familial, to inter-personal relationships. The irrational ideas associated with LFT also contribute to anger.

Returning to the core irrational belief associated with LFT ("Things have to be easy"), it is not difficult to see how such thinking contributes to anger. This idea is irrational for several reasons:

1. Things don't *have to be* any different than they happen to be.
2. Demanding things be easy will not make them easy.

3. Rather than being easy, many things in life are quite difficult.

Waters (1980) has stated that children are not born with the ability to tolerate frustration. Like most things, it has to be learned. Parents who rush in to rescue their children are doing them a disservice. They are robbing their children of the opportunity to learn how to delay gratification and tolerate frustration. Some have called these parents "helicopters" because they appear to be continually hovering above the child.

An interesting dynamic is that these same parents also seem to suffer from LFT. Why would a parent rush to rescue a child from an uncomfortable situation? Because it is easier to take care of the problem for the child than listen to him or her whine and complain. However, these parents are setting the stage for later problems by raising children who never acquire frustration tolerance. Parents struggle to control the behavior of a seven-year-old; wait until that child is fifteen. These same parents will look back on times when the child was seven as "the good old days." Since tolerating frustration has to be learned, there are techniques that can be beneficial in helping students develop this skill.

METHODS OF INCREASING FRUSTRATION TOLERANCE

1. *Help children determine if their frustration is caused by something they can change.* If frustration is caused by something that can be changed and children would like the situation altered, then by all means encourage them to make whatever changes are possible. If the situation is not something that can be changed, help them understand and accept this.

Children may feel that their lives would be much more enjoyable if they could somehow not be required to take math. However, math is a subject they will have to take for the next several years no matter how much they dislike it. The wise thing to do would be to accept this fact and figure out ways to make math more bearable.

2. *Continually point out the benefits of tolerating frustration.* As a child psychologist, I have a job that allows me to play with kids most of the day. A student actually turned to me in the middle of a group

counseling session one day and asked, "Where do you work?" It never dawned on him that what I was doing was actually my job!

I am able to do this because I tolerated the necessary headaches to get a graduate degree in psychology. Often I point this out to my clients, especially the older ones who are thinking about dropping out of school. Success often has less to do with intelligence than with the ability to tolerate frustration.

3. *Help children understand that nothing has to go their way just because they want it to.*

4. *Help children understand that almost nothing is a catastrophe.* There are lots of hassles, but few catastrophes. Some things are unfortunate and difficult, but we can stand anything. To believe that being called a name is a catastrophe is exaggerating the negative consequences of an event.

5. *Verbally praise students for their attempts to tolerate frustration.* Students have to be willing to try to tolerate frustration before they will master it. Praise these attempts whenever possible, even if they are unsuccessful.

6. *When students do exhibit LFT, point out the consequences of their choices.* If students don't study for exams and do poorly, make the association between their poor grades and their decision to go to the movies rather than study. Young people have the ability to ignore the real reasons for their failures and rationalize excuses. Don't let them off the hook that easily. By pointing out the relationship between their LFT and their difficulties, you can help them start to connect their difficulties with their LFT and make better choices in the future.

CONCLUSION

Anger is not caused by frustration, as many would suggest, but rather by the *demand* that one not be frustrated. Rational-Emotive Behavior Therapy places primary importance on thoughts, beliefs, and evaluations as the major determinant of emotional response. In other words, "People feel how they think."

It is appropriate to have negative emotions (sadness, irritation, etc.), but the goal is to feel an appropriate level of emotional intensity for the situation at hand. The primary belief leading to anger is that, "People or things should/must/have to/ought to be the way I want them to be!!" All anger is grandiosity because it involves taking personal preferences and turning them into universal commandments.

LFT is caused by the erroneous belief that, "My life must be completely free of all hassles." Such thinking causes a great many problems for children and adolescents.

The Differences between REBT and Other Approaches

A multitude of therapeutic approaches available today are designed to help individuals overcome personal difficulties. There are literally hundreds of schools of psychotherapy. Although it is beyond the scope of this book to examine all the various treatments, in this chapter a brief analysis is offered of a few of the most popular models of treatment. More specifically, various treatment models are compared and contrasted with REBT, the approach described throughout this book.

PSYCHOANALYSIS

Psychoanalysis was originated by Sigmund Freud during the early part of the twentieth century. His influence in the field of psychotherapy is still considerable. Psychoanalysis is the benchmark against which all other theories are measured.

The Freudian view of human nature is largely deterministic. Freud believed that people are primarily controlled by unconscious motivations and instinctual drives rather than by conscious thought. Psychoanalytic doctrines state that individuals become disturbed due to unresolved conflicts that occur during the first few years of life. Many of these conflicts involve sexual and aggressive motivations that have been repressed.

Psychoanalytic theories regarding the nature of emotional disturbance have been disputed by REBT practitioners. Ellis (1962) has continually maintained that individuals behave in given ways due to their thoughts, beliefs, and overall philosophies of life and not because of early experiences. Freudian doctrines regarding the importance of early experiences in personality development are in large part responsible for the widely held belief that "the past remains all important in my current life." However, according to REBT practitioners, what individuals are thinking in the present is much more important than what happened during their infancy. This theory maintains that if children have problems with anger it is not because they were emotionally neglected as infants and are unconsciously projecting their anger at their parents onto all adults. Rather, children are angry because they are currently demanding that they not be ignored. Children and adults convince themselves that others *must* treat them well or that things *should* be different. Their anger is a direct result of this tendency to demand command over things they do not control.

BEHAVIOR THERAPY

Behavioral theory was first developed by learning theorists such as E. L. Thorndike but was made popular by the work of psychologists such as Arnold Lazarus and B. F. Skinner. Behavior theory states that people are controlled by the influences of their environment. Behavior is the result of the rewards and punishments people have received during the course of their lives.

Rational-Emotive Behavior Therapy also disagrees with dogmatic behavioral theory, which views people as slaves to their environment. Obviously, children are influenced by the consequences they receive from their environment. However, it is the evaluation of these consequences that determines whether the outcomes are viewed as rewarding or punishing. To illustrate this point, let us use the example of recess again.

A child staying in from recess is not necessarily being penalized even though punishment may be the intent of the teacher. Whether staying in from recess is a reward or punishment depends on the child's beliefs, attitudes, and evaluations of this particular recess. If staying in from recess kept the child away from a student who had threatened to physically harm the child, the event would be reinforcing rather than punishing. It is always important to keep this in mind when developing behavioral plans for children. There are "hidden reinforcers" in many situations.

Behavior theory holds that a child has a problem with anger because he or she has been positively and negatively reinforced for becoming angry in the past. Although this is fundamentally correct, it is oversimplified in that it deals only with the observable behavior and fails to recognize the cause of the anger, which is the irrational demand made by the child.

A behavioral approach to reducing anger would reinforce a child for controlling his or her anger by rewarding the child with extended curfews, special privileges, or other luxuries. Punishment could be administered when a child exhibits angry and aggressive behavior. Such approaches often work, and they are used as part of REBT. However, used exclusively, strict behavioral approaches are often inefficient because they are concerned with the behavioral manifestations of anger and ignore the root of the problem, namely the irrational beliefs associated with anger. It is more effective to directly attack the self-defeating, illogical ideas that cause anger. Also, when students understand the cognitive roots of their anger, they are in a much better position to be able to generalize from the treatment setting to real world applications.

When behavioral approaches are successful, they work because the interventions (i.e., the administration of rewards and punishers) have brought about changes in the child's thinking. It is better to set up a treatment plan that includes a cognitive component because irrational cognitions are the cause of the problem in the first place.

CLIENT-CENTERED THERAPY

A client-centered approach to anger control focuses on providing the client with unconditional love and acceptance. By forming a positive relationship with the therapist, children can begin to value and accept themselves. Client-centered approaches rely on the belief that the answers to problems must be found by the clients. These insights will be discovered when children are ready. The therapist's job is to support the client in this search for understanding.

Although REBT theory agrees that unconditional acceptance of a client is desirable, REBT practitioners do not consider the relationship between the student and the therapist to be all important. The idea, "Because my counselor values me, I am a valuable person," is highly irrational. A counselor's opinion of a client has nothing to do with the client's inherent value as a human being. Such ideas can foster dependent relationships between the client and therapist that will interfere with the goals of therapy.

In client-centered therapy, children can receive a confusing message regarding their behavior and their inherent value. It is difficult for children to understand that there is a difference between their behavior and who they are as people. The idea that others can be displeased with their behavior but still unconditionally accept them is difficult for children to understand. It is better to explain to children that being angry is okay, but being violent is not. They have the right, as fallible human beings, to make mistakes, but there will be very real consequences of their choices.

Rational-Emotive Behavior Therapy also disagrees with the idea that clients can only gain real insight into their difficulties if they are allowed to discover their own insights. Waiting for children to come up with the understanding to act in a healthier manner may take years and in some cases may never happen at all. The fact that clients in this situation are children makes it even more unlikely that there will be meaningful insight into a problem. Ellis (1962) has pointed out that even after insights are made, many clients continue to act in the same disturbed manner.

PRIMAL SCREAM THERAPY

In primal scream therapy, clients are encouraged to scream to get out their anger. Primal scream therapy supports the notion that releasing anger is healthy and that by expressing rage, children and adolescents will feel less angry in the future.

The idea that by venting pent-up feelings of rage clients will be less hostile in similar situations may sound logical. However, research does not support this contention. Several studies have shown that when subjects release their anger toward others, they often become *more*, rather than *less*, irate. Berkowitz (1970) conducted a study in which frustrated subjects in one group were allowed to strike the agitator, and subjects in another group were prevented from doing so. The subjects who were allowed to act aggressively were just as likely to become angry under similar circumstances in the future.

Feshbach (1971) conducted a study in which subjects had their ability to act aggressively inhibited. The direct inhibition of aggressive behavior actually reduced aggression in the subjects. The author noted that acknowledging and labeling the emotion (anger) appeared to provide sufficient expression in most instances, and overt expression of anger no longer appeared to be necessary.

What is most unfortunate about the primal scream school of therapy is that not only does this treatment fail to reduce hostility, it actually reinforces anger. It also inadvertently reinforces the irrational idea that "Life has to treat me fairly." In reality, there is not one reason why life has to be any more fair than it is at this moment. People have the right to demand that the world treat them fairly, but it is ridiculous to believe that anyone else *should* care that things haven't gone to their liking.

INNER CHILD THERAPY

In recent years there has been an increase in therapeutic approaches that focus on "nurturing the inner child." Many of these approaches include provocative and unusual treatments. After returning from a residential treatment facility, one of my former clients carried around a teddy bear that symbolized his inner child. This eighteen-year-old took his teddy bear with him everywhere he went and, of course, was even more ostracized by his classmates. Many have watched the proliferation of these therapies with shock and disbelief.

The public has always had a hunger for this type of "voodoo" psychological treatment because people have always wanted to find magic in the universe. They want to believe that there is a special therapy that can go back to when they were infants and "fix" their troubled pasts. Some practitioners in the mental health profession have a vested interest in perpetuating this silliness. The profession wants the public to keep believing that therapists have fairy dust or some secret potion to cure what ails them.

The reality is that there is no magic or fairy dust in the universe. If clients are going to get better at managing their anger, it will come from changing what they are thinking. They have every right to carry around teddy bears, drink from baby bottles, or perform other rituals and incantations. However, this type of behavior won't help them learn to cope with their anger. Granted, it sometimes feels good for students to vent about their situation, but it usually does very little to help them cope more effectively in their daily lives. That comes through a philosophical change, which unfortunately is hard work and takes a lot of practice. If clients believe that therapy should be fun, they may very well be disappointed.

RATIONAL-EMOTIVE BEHAVIOR THERAPY

The originator of REBT is Albert Ellis, a New York psychologist who was originally trained as a psychoanalyst. Ellis became dissatisfied with classic psychoanalysis as a means of treatment. On several occasions he has stated that he appears to have been born with a "gene for efficiency" and thus abandoned traditional analysis for the following reasons:

1. Psychoanalysis takes a considerable amount of time. Often patients are in treatment literally for years.
2. One of the cardinal tenets of analysis is "with insight comes cure." That is, once clients understand the nature of the conflict, they will be able to overcome their difficulties. As mentioned previously, Ellis (1962) found that even after clients had apparently gained insight into their problem, they continued to act in the same unhealthy manner.
3. Although some clients improve under psychoanalytic treatment, very few improve substantially.

In the spring of 1955, Ellis began experimenting with new techniques such as having the client sit upright rather than lie on a couch, the common practice in traditional psychoanalysis. However, many of the problems associated with traditional psychoanalysis (such as the three just listed) also plagued his face-to-face psychoanalysis.

Ellis also began to be more active and directive with his clients. Rather than waiting for them to gain insight into the nature of a conflict, he would directly point out the inconsistencies in their reasoning. Ellis commented, "Much to my surprise, this more superficial method actually started to produce not only quicker but apparently deeper and more lasting effects" (1962, p. 8).

In the first outcome study using this new method of psychotherapy, which came to be called Rational-Emotive Therapy (RET), Ellis (1957) compared RET, orthodox psychoanalysis, and what he referred to as psychoanalytically oriented (PAO) therapy, face-to-face analysis. Ellis compared seventy-eight cases using RET with PAO, the sample being composed of sixty-one neurotics and seventeen borderline psychotics. Twelve neurotics and four borderline psychotics were treated using orthodox psychoanalysis. The number of treatments using RET, PAO, and orthodox analysis were twenty-six, thirty-five, and ninety-three, respectively. Ellis rated each case as showing 1) little or no progress, 2) some improvement, or 3) considerable improvement. Using orthodox psychoanalysis, 50 percent showed little or no improvement, 37 percent showed some improvement, and 13 percent showed considerable improvement. Using PAO, 37 percent demonstrated little or no improvement, 45 percent showed some improvement, and 18 percent showed considerable improvement. Using RET, the results appeared to be superior: only 10 percent showed little or no improvement, while 46 percent had some improvement, and 44 percent demonstrated considerable improvement.

Ellis initially called this new approach Rational Therapy, but the label led some to believe that the sole emphasis in this new form of therapy was on cognitions (Dryden, 1990). Ellis has always maintained that cognitions, emotions, and behavior are interrelated. He wanted his new form of therapy to emphasize all three components and their interactions. The name was changed in 1961 to Rational-Emotive Therapy (RET) to avoid incorrect associations with the philosophical approach known as rationalism, which RET opposed. Ellis argued that RET could have been known as rational-emotive behavioral therapy because

RET also encourages its clients to behaviorally practice their new beliefs, so in 1993 he officially changed the name to Rational-Emotive Behavior Therapy (REBT).

Ellis (1985) claimed to have developed the basic principles of REBT as he worked on overcoming his own anxieties. He used to be quite shy, especially around females. He decided that to overcome his anxiety he would approach 100 women outside the Bronx Botanical Gardens over a period of one month. Ellis reported that he actually approached more than a hundred women but was largely rebuffed by those he tried to speak with. He managed to get one date, but the woman failed to show up at their arranged meeting time. Although he did not meet many women through his experiment, Ellis found that he lost any fear of talking to them. Once he did what he previously feared doing, his anxiety quickly disappeared.

Ellis (1962; 1973) has stated that emotional suffering is largely caused by illogical and irrational beliefs that people hold. He has examined twelve major irrational beliefs, which are discussed below along with their rational alternatives.

1. *The idea that you must—yes, must—have sincere love and approval all the time from all the people you find significant* instead of the rational idea that no one *has to* have what he or she wants, including love and approval. As infants, people are dependent on the care of others for survival. Some people hold onto this dependency well past infancy, even into adulthood, and maintain that humans *need* love. Although it is true that almost all people would like and prefer to have love, no one *needs* love to survive. Love is essentially someone else's opinion, and people can choose to either agree or disagree with that opinion.

Trying to be loved and approved of by everyone is not only unrealistic and unobtainable but will cause individuals to waste a good deal of time and energy (Wilde, 1992). Clients who accept themselves regardless of other's opinions are much more likely to live with minimum amounts of anger, anxiety, and depression.

2. *The idea that you must prove yourself thoroughly competent, adequate, and achieving, or that you must at least have real competence or talent at something important* rather than the rational idea that *doing* is more important than *doing well*. People have a multitude of skills

and abilities. Succeeding does not make an individual worthwhile; failing does not make an individual worthless.

A very clear message supported by American society is that children's worth can somehow be measured or proven by the level of success they obtain in various endeavors. Many people mistakenly consider the idea of accepting people as inherently worthwhile no matter what their achievement to be conceited and wrong. It is much more logical to accept individuals as inherently valuable and worthwhile rather than associating their value with their accomplishments. People are far too complicated to obtain ratings regarding their successes or failures in all the facets of their life. Even if this were possible, who does the rating? Who would determine which facets are most important? Are mechanical skills more important than talents in investing, for example?

3. *The idea that people who harm you or commit misdeeds are inherently bad, wicked, or villainous individuals and that you should severely blame, damn, and punish them for their sins* rather than the rational idea that everyone makes mistakes. It makes no sense to blame others for their mistakes because all humans are fallible. To expect people to be mistake-free is a failure to accept reality. It is better to appreciate the fact that people are free to act in any manner they desire even if other people may not understand or appreciate their behavior. As fallible beings, people have the right to act badly at times.

4. *The idea that life is awful, terrible, horrible, and catastrophic when things do not go the way you would like them to go* rather than the rational idea that many things are inconveniences but very few are catastrophes. When words like "terrible," "awful," and "horrible" are emotionally translated, they mean "worse than 100 percent bad," which is impossible. There are many undesirable events, but nothing is so bad that it cannot be tolerated. This may seem to be counterintuitive, but it is true. Even death will be "tolerated" someday. When that time eventually comes, all will "stand" death whether they like it or not.

It is possible to exaggerate the "badness" of an event into an apocalyptic catastrophe and create unneeded anxiety. Things rarely go perfectly, yet most people find a moderate amount of happiness despite the imperfect nature of the world. Even though things occasionally go wrong, it is still not a catastrophe, just an unfortunate reality.

5. *The idea that emotional misery comes from external pressures and that you have little ability to control your feelings or rid yourself of depression and hostility* rather than the rational idea that individuals feel how they think and, therefore, have tremendous control over their emotions. When clients believe that others have the power to make them angry, they grant these people control over their lives. The fact remains that people are responsible for their own feelings. No one is a puppet to be manipulated with strings by an evil puppet master.

The understanding that people have a significant influence over the emotions they feel takes away the possibility of blaming others for their unhappiness. Such beliefs are threatening to clients intent on blaming their current situation on circumstances beyond their control.

6. *The idea that if something seems dangerous or fearsome, you must be terribly occupied with and upset about it* rather than the rational idea that worrying about an event will not keep the event from occurring. If the feared event does transpire, it will be "standable" but perhaps not enjoyable. One can learn to accept the inevitable, no matter what that might be.

7. *The idea that you will find it easier to avoid facing many of life's difficulties and self-responsibilities than to undertake some form of self-discipline* rather than the rational idea that the "easy way" is invariably much harder in the long run (Trimpey, 1992). Facing a difficult situation head on is often the best way to deal with the problem and be done with it.

Problems rarely improve or go away spontaneously. It usually takes a concerted effort to improve one's lot in life.

8. *The idea that your past remains all important and that, because something once strongly influenced your life, it has to keep determining your feelings and behavior today* rather than the rational idea that the past has an influence over the present but does not determine the here and now. *We now feel the way we now think.*

The past does not really exist except in memories, and those memories are only impressions of the past as it was then seen. It is also true that these memories are substantially influenced by our interpretations and selective attention to those events. There is no such thing as objective history, because each individual will create his or her own interpretation of the past. The most important point is that humans have the ability to change no matter what the past was like.

9. *The idea that people and things should turn out better than they do, and that you have to view it as awful and horrible if you do not quickly find good solutions to life's hassles* rather than the rational idea that there is absolutely no evidence that anything *should* be different than it actually happens to be.

Everything is as it should be now. If all the prerequisites that were necessary for an event to transpire have occurred, then the event *must* happen. For example, for there to be a flu epidemic, certain prerequisites must have been met. Whatever those prerequisites were (such as the existence of a flu virus, exposure to the virus, and a weakened immune system that cannot fight off the virus), they have occurred. If they have occurred, not only *should* there be a flu epidemic, but logically there *must* be a flu epidemic.

Sometimes people believe that the word "should" carries moral overtones. In REBT, this is not intended. "There should be a flu epidemic this year," does not imply that a flu epidemic would be a good thing. In REBT, such a statement merely conveys the fact that if all the prerequisites for an event to transpire have occurred, then the event must occur.

10. *The idea that you can achieve happiness by inertia and inaction or by passively and uncommittedly "enjoying yourself"* rather than the rational idea that humans tend to be happiest when creatively absorbed in some type of enjoyable activity and devoted to projects outside themselves. Individuals who passively take part in life rarely lead rewarding lives. People tend to be the happiest when they are engaged in activities they value.

11. *The idea that you must have a high degree of order or certainty to feel comfortable, or that you need some supernatural power on which to rely* rather than the rational idea that very few certainties, if any, exist in the universe. It is quite possible to be relatively happy most of the time.

Some people may have a desire for a supernatural power to rely on, but many individuals appear to get along without believing in a higher power. Even if such a power did not exist, life could still be meaningful and enjoyable. The lack of a belief in a supernatural power does not guarantee a meaningless existence.

12. *The idea that you can give yourself a global rating as a human and that your general self-worth and self-acceptance depend on the quality of your performance and the degree to which people approve of you* rather than the rational idea that human beings are too complex to be given an overall rating. All humans are a combination of both positive and negative traits. It is best if clients can simply accept themselves as inherently valuable, because it is not possible to either prove or disprove inherent value. All human beings are enormously valuable and worthwhile to themselves because they are the only ones who can act in a manner to satisfy their desires. As has been stated previously, successes do not make people worthwhile, and failures do not make people worthless.

THE PHILOSOPHY OF REBT

Rational-Emotive Behavior Therapy theory states that humans are basically hedonistic: They attempt to stay alive, seek pleasure, and avoid pain. The therapy does not support irresponsible behavior that might sacrifice long-term happiness for immediate gratification. To live for today is desirable, but not at the expense of tomorrow. Therefore, REBT supports responsible hedonism because people live in a social world, and their self-interests ideally will make the world a better place to live in or at least not infringe on others' pursuit of happiness.

Rational-Emotive Behavior Therapy encourages the use of the scientific method to gather information and make decisions. Walen, DiGiuseppe, and Wessler (1980) stated that the methods of science are the best methods for learning about ourselves, others, and the world. The scientific method begins with a hypothesis and proceeds by searching for evidence to support the hypothesis. If evidence can be found supporting a hypothesis or belief, the belief is said to be rational.

Therapists using REBT encourage their clients to put their interests first most of the time and the interests of others a close second. Sacrificing personal desires to meet the desires of others is not encouraged unless clients want to sacrifice themselves and find happiness in doing so.

Some have criticized REBT for teaching clients to be selfish, but REBT does not support infringing on the rights of others to satisfy personal desires. It merely states that individuals should make certain that their desires are met because no one else is responsible for ensuring their happiness and satisfaction. In other words, no one else can *make* them happy. As stated previously, all humans are abundantly worthwhile to themselves because no one else has the power to produce feelings of happiness and satisfaction in them.

Rational-Emotive Behavior Theory states that people are natural philosophers. In the entire animal kingdom, humans are the only species with the unique ability to think about their thinking. Our philosophies about ourselves and our world have a significant influence on our feelings and behaviors. In turn, our feelings and behaviors can have an influence on our philosophies. The best way to eliminate or avoid unnecessary pain and suffering in life is through a basic philosophical change. If children can be assisted in changing their irrational beliefs from absolute demands to preferences, from catastrophes to inconveniences, and from self-denigration to self-acceptance, they will be in a much better position to enjoy life (Wilde, 1995b).

CONCLUSION: OVERVIEW OF COUNSELING MODELS

Psychoanalysis

The focus in psychoanalysis is on unconscious drives as the determinants of behavior. Attention is given to early events (i.e., the first six years of life) as being of primary importance in later personality development.

Behavior Therapy

Behavior therapy focuses on the rewards and punishments the client receives from the environment. These factors shape behavior.

Client-Centered Therapy

The relationship between the client and counselor is of primary importance. Through the therapist's empathetic understanding and unconditional acceptance, clients are inspired to accept themselves.

Primal Scream Therapy

Primal scream places emphasis on the expression of anger as a means of opening the client to new experiences and ameliorating the effects of anger.

Inner Child Therapy

This therapy employs provocative, psychodramatic techniques designed to allow clients to work through earlier traumatic experiences. Advocates believe that it is necessary to emotionally "relive" earlier traumas to be able to move beyond these roadblocks to growth.

Rational-Emotive Behavior Therapy

This therapy places primary importance on cognition as the determinant of emotion. It postulates that irrational thoughts, typically in the form of dogmatic beliefs and overgeneralizations, are responsible for emotional disturbance.

CHAPTER 6

Setting the Stage for Change

Before therapy sessions begin there are several factors that require consideration to maximize the effectiveness of the interventions. Counselors best not forget about some of the preparatory, yet meaningful, elements leading to successful treatment.

REFERRALS: SELF VERSUS OTHER

An important distinction should be made between adult and child clients. These two categories of clients differ in significant ways, and it is beyond the scope of this book to thoroughly examine this issue. This chapter focuses on the difference between self and "other" (e.g., teacher, principal) referrals.

A majority of adult clients are in therapy voluntarily. Even in cases in which adults are not self-referrals, they are still attending sessions by their own choosing. A husband may be attending counseling at the request of his wife, but he still is making a conscious decision to participate in the therapeutic process, even if this choice is primarily motivated by his desire to please his wife or avoid her wrath.

Children, on the other hand, are typically not self-referrals. It is rare for a child with an anger problem to seek assistance voluntarily. This is not surprising considering some of the core irrational beliefs held by clients with anger problems. These beliefs almost always demand something from an external source. The problem is rarely internal—it is with the rest of the world. These students seem to believe, "The world should shape up and get in line with my demands!" Angry students will insist that the school, parents, and/or police are the problem, and that if everyone else would change, there would be nothing to be concerned about.

Most clients with anger problems are referred by school personnel such as teachers and administrators. The referral may come from the parent, but it is usually initiated by the school unless the child has been exhibiting significant behavior problems at home and in the community.

The referring party usually does not understand the nature of psychotherapy and just wants some relief from the problems the client has been causing. This can involve another problem—the public's desire for magic. People are under the mistaken impression that counselors have the power to *change* clients. The message counselors typically receive from teachers or parents is, "Fix him!" or "Fix her!" They don't care how it is done, just so it *is* done.

When the referral is made, the counselor should have a brief discussion with whomever referred the student. Counselors are free to ignore this suggestion if they have unlimited time on their hands and enjoy counseling hostile, resistant adolescents!

Make it a point to ask if the student has expressed an interest in learning to control his or her anger. This will open an opportunity to explain that unless the client wants to change, it is difficult to make progress. It's sort of like that old joke, "How many counselors does it take to change a light bulb?" Answer: "One, but the light bulb has to be willing to change." There is a lot of truth in that joke.

Even if the referring party states that the student doesn't view the situation as his or her problem, it is still advisable to interview the client to assess the situation. Although the client may be placing responsibility for the problem on others, there are interventions designed to convince a student that learning to manage anger may be in his or her best interests.

HELPING CLIENTS OWN THE PROBLEM

One of the ways to encourage clients to commit to changing is to help them comprehend all the ways in which anger is causing problems in their lives. Most of these clients are already involved with the school's disciplinary procedures and may also have contact with the juvenile authorities. Try to make the connection between their difficulties and their uncontrolled temper.

Glenn, an eighth-grade student, was having a difficult year. He was the type of student who had always had a few problems during the year, but nothing serious. During his eighth-grade year, Glenn seemed to spiral out of control. On two occasions the police had to be summoned to the school, and Glenn was charged with disorderly conduct. He also had been involved in several crimes over the summer, including assault and stealing a van. As his problems began to mount, the principal asked me if I had time to work with him to see if there was anything more the school could do to help.

Therapist: Let me ask you something. Are you having problems in school as far as detentions and stuff like that?

Glenn: Yeah. I've got two Saturday detentions.

T: Two?

G: Yeah.

T: What did you do to get those?

G: I walked out of Mr. Weith's class. For that I got one DT and I got the other one for not serving that DT last Saturday.

T: Why did you walk out of Mr. Weith's class?

G: I had a report to give and I wasn't ready so I asked if I could give it the next day and he said, "No."

T: And you did what?

G: I called him a name and walked out.

T: Think back to that time and tell me, what were you feeling?

G: I was pissed off. John's report wasn't until the next day, but he was ready, so I asked if John could take my place and I could take his.

T: So you were angry that Mr. Weith wouldn't let you switch?

G: Yeah.

T: Do you think you would have gotten detention if you hadn't gotten angry?

G: I don't know.

T: What's you're best guess?

G: Probably not.

T: Why not?

G: Because I wouldn't have had a reason to call him a name.

T: I think you're probably right. You get along pretty good with Mr. Weith. The problems start when you get angry and start making some poor decisions. We do some pretty stupid stuff when we get angry, don't we? Or at least I do. Why did you get the second DT?

(Author's note—I knew why he got the second detention but I had the feeling that it might be related to his temper again.)

G: Because I didn't serve the first one.

T: That's right. I remember now. Why didn't you?

G: I was going to but it was a really nice day and I thought, "This really sucks" and I just blew it off.

T: Let me guess something: You were going to go but then you started thinking about it and you got mad all over again and made another poor decision. Is that right?

G: Yeah, pretty much.

T: I think I see a pattern here. When you get mad you do things that wind you up in trouble. Now because of your anger you've got to spend the next two Saturday mornings in school.

G: It sucks.

T: Do you think that if you could learn not to get angry you'd spend less time in trouble?

G: Probably.

At this point there is at least a window of opportunity provided by the client to explore the problem. The first step (i.e., getting the client to take responsibility for the problem) may have been accomplished, but there is a second hurdle to clear.

Even if clients readily admit that their anger is a significant problem, they must be willing to work hard between sessions. Many clients seem to have the attitude, "I'm willing to change if changing will be easy." Unfortunately, that is not an option. Changing established behavior patterns is almost never easy. In fact, it is almost always quite difficult. Human beings are creatures of habit, and once a habit is established there are psychological and biological factors that keep the pattern reoccurring.

Psychologically, the irrational beliefs that produce anger occur at a level below a client's awareness. These beliefs are usually not noticed by the student. Ask a client, "What were you thinking right before you made yourself angry?" and a common response is, "I wasn't thinking anything." Inexperienced counselors may take this response as a form of malingering or resistance, but most often the client is just being honest. He or she isn't aware of the thoughts that precede the anger. These cognitions occur almost automatically. One can easily see why changing a habit that is triggered by thoughts that occur automatically would be difficult.

Biologically, once a habit is established the neuronal connections associated with that habit are strengthened each time the thought or behavior is carried out. These dendritic connections operate with increasing efficiency, and they become more difficult to reroute the longer the pattern has occurred.

THE IMPORTANCE OF PRACTICE

Clients have the mistaken impression that therapy consists of talking once in a while; then the problem goes away. Do everything you can to impress upon your clients that if they want to improve at anything, they need to practice. If someone wants to become a better roller skater, for example, the only way to achieve that goal is to practice. A person could spend all day thinking about how much he or she wants to be a better roller skater, but unless he or she actually gets out and roller skates, he or she won't improve. It is the same way with learning how to control one's temper. People can want to do so with all their hearts, but wanting alone won't make it happen.

The other analogy I use is that of a coach and an athlete. The coach can tell an athlete how to train and what to do, but the athlete is the one who has to do the work. The greatest coach in the world can't help an athlete who won't train. It's a waste of time for both the coach and the athlete.

A technique I use to assess clients' willingness to work involves a cassette tape and worksheet. The tape is about twenty minutes in length and contains information regarding REBT. The tape is a good way of reinforcing some of the REBT concepts that usually are presented in the first session. However, my primary reason for using the tape and worksheet is to assess clients' motivation.

Clients are instructed to listen to the tape and answer the questions on the worksheet before the next session. The questions are very easy to answer if clients simply listen to the tape. If the following week arrives and clients have not completed the worksheet, it is a good indication that they are unmotivated and unwilling to practice. If this occurs I use the opportunity to reemphasize the importance of practicing. If clients won't take the time to listen to a short tape, it leads me to believe they aren't very interested in practicing.

School counselors, psychologists, and social workers always seem to have more potential clients than they can serve. Things like the tape and worksheet can help determine which clients are ready to work and which are not. That is not to say that clients who aren't ready to work won't become unhappy enough in the future to be ready for therapy. It is essential for mental health professionals to maximize their effectiveness because there are so many children needing help. Strike while the iron is hot; find the clients who are ready to work.

If you have worked with clients for a session or two and they give no indication of being ready for therapy, it may be appropriate to discontinue treatment temporarily. It is important that these clients know that your door is always open when they are interested in working with you. I usually tell clients something along these lines:

> I don't think it's a good time for us to work together because I'm not certain you're ready to learn how to manage your anger. I don't think you want to change and I'm not going to try and make you do something you don't want to do. I haven't seen you making any real effort with the ideas I've been asking you to practice. It's hard work to change and it will take a lot of my time and your time. Right now I think we'd be wasting each other's time. When you want to work at learning how not to become angry, come and see me.

Occasionally a confrontation will energize clients. It makes them realize the seriousness of the sessions. At other times it helps them understand why you will not be seeing them individually in the weeks to come.

One of the things that never ceases to amaze me is how much time and pain it takes before people are ready to change. Some clients are more difficult than others, and clients with anger problems can be quite stubborn. Unfortunately, the only way some people learn is through pain. When clients are about to expelled from school, thrown out of their homes, put into a lock-up facility, or face some other major consequence, expect to find them knocking at your door. This discomfort can serve them well because through their pain they can become very motivated learners. Pain can be a good thing. We have pain to help us understand when it is time for a change. Emotional pain only becomes a significant problem when it is continually ignored.

A client I saw several years ago was referred to me by his parents. He was seeing a psychiatrist in another city due to difficulties with depression. We talked for about thirty minutes, and I gave him a copy of the tape and worksheet and asked him to complete it before the next week's session. A couple of hours later I was checking my mailbox at the high school and the tape and completed worksheet were there. This client had listened to the tape and worksheet over his lunch hour. Obviously the client was very motivated, and we started working together immediately. If he was given a homework assignment to practice his rational coping statements for five minutes, three times a day, he would practice them for ten minutes, five times a day. He improved dramatically and was able to be taken off antidepressants in a short period of time. He may have been so motivated because he disliked the side effects of the medication.

If you are not comfortable with a tape and worksheet, develop some other screening device to help you determine which clients are ready to work. Again, the answers on the worksheet are not as important as the effort used to complete it. (I'd be happy to send you a copy of the tape and sheet I use if you'll send me a self-addressed, stamped envelope and a blank cassette tape. The address is given in chapter 14.)

ELEMENTARY VERSUS SECONDARY

Clients from different grade levels have various capabilities, and your approach must address these differences. Elementary and secondary students differ in their ability to use abstract reasoning and language skills. These differences have a profound influence on the nature of the therapeutic process.

Rational-Emotive Behavior Therapy has been criticized by some as only being effective with brighter students. Some have even mistakenly stated that REBT cannot be used effectively with elementary students. Although these assertions are incorrect, it is true that the cognitive limitations of clients should be taken into consideration. It is foolish to think that all clients can be treated in the same manner. If a student is not an abstract thinker, it would be inappropriate to rely on abstract principles as a primary means of disputing and changing his or her irrational beliefs. Most seven-year-olds would be unable to grasp the notion that it is irrational to say a parent *should not* have withheld their allowance. It is irrational because all of the events necessary to have the allowance withheld did transpire. First, the client had to break some type of rule (for example, not cleaning her room), which she did. Second, the parents had to catch her in the act, which they did. Third, the parents had to decide that this violation warranted a punishment, which they did. Last, the parents had to inform the child that she would not be receiving her allowance for the week, which they did. Therefore, the parents *should* have acted exactly the way they did because that is how they did act!

This same seven-year-old could probably understand that it would be better to *wish* that she had not lost her allowance, but to demand that she not have the money withheld is silly because parents make the rules, not the kids. If the child thinks she has the power to control her parents, have her try to convince her parents to paint the house in polka dots.

Adolescents are different animals in many important ways. They are often confusing because they resemble a walking, talking paradox. Consider the following examples of their apparently contradictory nature:

1. Teenagers tend to be very egocentric and believe that the world should be as they want it to be. Although they may possess physical maturity, they have not had sufficient life experience to understand or appreciate perspectives different from their own.
2. Adolescents tend to be insecure regarding their own skills and abilities, but many try desperately to hide these insecurities. Males often hide behind a mask of macho bravado.

3. Teenagers are overly sensitive and have their feelings hurt easily due to their inner focus. The slightest look or wrong word can have a devastating effect on their feelings of self-worth.
4. Because they do not have a clear sense of who they are, adolescents tend to define themselves through their group affiliations. It is also common for adolescents to see themselves according to how others define them.
5. Teenagers tend to experience mood swings and will go from elation to depression in a matter of minutes. To predict why this happens or when it will occur is nearly impossible.
6. Adolescents constantly worry about being too much like everyone else, so they strive for their own look and ideas. Conversely, they dislike being singled out as being too different.
7. Adolescents are embarrassed by their parents yet depend heavily on them.
8. Many teenagers have social anxiety and find it easier to withdraw from social contact, even though by doing so they may be missing enjoyable activities.

SUGGESTIONS FOR WORKING WITH ELEMENTARY-AGED CLIENTS

When working with elementary-aged students, try not to stare continuously at the child, especially during the initial session. Forget the idea that maintaining good eye contact is a way of showing clients that you have a real interest in what they are saying. Too much eye contact will make many children anxious. It is best to observe clients in short segments. This allows students to examine you and their surroundings.

With noticeably anxious children, it can be beneficial to allow them to perform some type of physical activity such as drawing or coloring. The use of art therapy has two advantages. Not only does it allow children to perform some physical activity to help them relax, it also can be used as a rich source of information. The interpretation of children's drawings can provide insight into the nature of the problem.

It is not advisable for counselors to adopt a "little persons" voice when working with younger students. Children will sense that there is something artificial about such a practice and feel uneasy. However, it is appropriate to become more childlike. Something I use that almost all my clients enjoy is a secret handshake. Kids really enjoy things like special greetings, and these procedures communicate to the child, "You can trust me because although I appear to be an adult, inside I'm still a kid."

Get on the child's level. If possible, get on the floor rather than a chair. If you have to sit at a table, try putting your hands flat on the table and your chin on your hands. This usually will put the counselor below the client. Children seem to open up when adults adopt this passive posture.

During the first session, try not to overwhelm children with questions. At least ask open-ended questions that will allow them to elaborate and get used to hearing their voices in the room. Too many questions can have a negative effect and cause a normally talkative child to become quiet. If possible, get background information about the child from others.

CONCLUSION

Many clients with anger problems are not self-referrals. For therapy to be effective, it is recommended that counselors try to help clients feel at least partially responsible for their feelings. The use of some type of informal procedure (e.g., a tape and worksheet) is a helpful way of assessing motivation to change and willingness to practice between sessions.

It is important to take into account developmental differences when working with elementary and secondary students. Secondary students have many paradoxical characteristics. It's important to help children feel comfortable during counseling sessions. Allowing them to draw or sit on the floor may help younger students relax.

CHAPTER 7

Techniques for Coping with Anger

Although anger can be thought of as resulting from some core irrational belief such as "Things should be as I want them to be," this belief has many derivatives. It produces anger that can be directed at various individuals or situations. Before turning our attention to interventions for anger-prone individuals, let's examine the individuals and situations that are likely to be the source, but not the cause, of students' anger.

EPISODES OF ANGER

Averill (1982; 1983) used college students and adults to examine episodes of anger. Although this book focuses on anger in children and adolescents, the information from Averill's studies is worth reviewing.

Averill's subjects reported that 75 percent of their anger was directed at a loved one, friend, or acquaintance. Eight percent was toward someone well-known and disliked, and 13 percent at a stranger. An overwhelming majority of anger (85 percent) was the result of being accused of committing some misdeed. Once they were angry, 60 percent of the subjects did something to calm themselves, and 59 percent reported talking over the incident. Direct physical aggression was reported only 10 percent of the time, but verbal or symbolic aggression was more common, at 44 percent.

As Averill's research indicated, the majority of anger is directed at others, but it can also be turned inward toward the self. Conversely, some individuals project anger nearly everywhere except at themselves.

ANGER AT OTHERS

It probably comes as no surprise that children and adolescents find it easy to make themselves angry at others. Ellis (1977a) and others (Grieger, 1982; Dryden, 1990) have pointed out that anger at others typically revolves around four themes. Anger occurs when others 1) block clients from achieving their goals, 2) attack clients or their values, 3) threaten clients, and 4) break clients' rules.

Anger from Blocked Goals

Mel, a seventeen-year-old senior, had a goal of graduating in the top 10 percent of his class. Whether he achieved this goal depended on his grade in a physics course. Mel felt fairly confident he would be able to receive an A- from Mr. Albright. He was certain Mr. Albright would give him the "benefit of the doubt."

When report cards came out Mel received a B + and found out later that he missed the A- by only a few points. He was infuriated that Mr. Albright wouldn't give him the grade he felt he deserved.

When working with some clients, it is difficult to reach agreement on the irrational belief causing their anger. In this case it was quite simple; within five minutes Mel had stated, "Mr. Albright ought to give me a break" and went on to explain how hard he had worked in Mr. Albright's class.

One of the goals of my first session with Mel was to show him that there really was no reason why Mr. Albright "ought to" give him a break just because he "could" give him a break. As Ellis has pointed out, many anger-prone individuals have the mistaken idea that because others *can* treat us well, they *should* treat us well.

By demanding that his wishes be granted, Mel was setting himself up to be angry. This is a classic example of an individual taking a strong wish and turning it into a demand.

Mel left after one session and did not return. He really wasn't interested in controlling his anger and simply wanted to complain about the poor treatment he felt he had received from Mr. Albright. He may have wanted me to intervene on his behalf, but I had no intention of putting myself in the middle of this situation. He might have been thinking, "Dr. Wilde *shouldn't* take the teacher's side."

Anger from Attacking Values

Gina, also a senior, was in one of the numerous support groups I facilitate at the high school. She was a foster child and had a lot of difficulties accepting the way her birth mother treated her. Gina put up with a long history of emotional and physical abuse before she was finally taken away from her mother by Child Protective Services workers.

She had just finished sharing an incident that took place several years earlier involving her mother when another group member made the comment, "Your mother sounds like a real ass." Gina immediately became very angry, which surprised the other group members. She had spent most of her time in group complaining about her mother and was now angry when another group member echoed her sentiments.

Having worked with numerous foster children, I was not surprised by her attitude. Many of these clients seem to have the belief that it is perfectly acceptable for them to say negative things about their parents. However, others had better not share a negative opinion, because they hadn't earned that right, so to speak.

After group, Gina and I talked about what had happened. I tried to explain to her that others have the right to think and say what they want about her, her mother, or anyone else. I agreed with her that it would be better if others didn't make negative comments about her mother, but that did not mean they *should* not. We proceeded to make a list of things that the world would be better off without, such as child abuse, drugs, and crime. But I also pointed out that even though most people would agree that the world would be a happier place if these problems didn't exist, there was still no reason that they *should not* or *must not* exist. I also tried to explain that not everyone shared her value of loyalty to the family and that her reaction was difficult for some of the group members to understand given the things she had said about her mother.

Anger from Threat

Wade had been dating Lyn for several months (which is a lifetime for high school students). He became upset when a student from a neighboring town asked her to his school's prom. Wade perceived this as a direct threat to his relationship with Lyn and made it known all over the school that if her suitor showed his face in town, there would be trouble.

The irrational belief producing Wade's anger was, "People have no right to ask out my girlfriend." A secondary belief that often accompanies such a demand has to do with the wickedness of an individual who dares to break such a commandment. Wade also believed that Lyn's friend was a "bastard" who "should have his butt kicked."

As mentioned previously, anger often interferes with the capability for rational or logical thought. It was difficult to get Wade to think through his idea that others have no right to ask out Lyn. Wade needed to accept the rational ideas that 1) Lyn is not married and 2) even if she were, others could still request her company, although a large percentage of society would consider it in poor taste, sinful, and inappropriate to do so. People have the right to have poor taste.

Anger from Broken Rules

Chapter 9 contains transcripts of three counseling sessions with John, who angered himself when others used foul language, breaking one of his "rules." It is important to note that the content of the client's rules is not important. What is important is that the rule has been broken. The rule could be, "No one is allowed to wear green socks on Friday," or some other ridiculous demand. When students set up dogmatic rules for the rest of the universe, they are bound to be angry because others will not necessarily share their values and will break those rules.

ANGER AT SELF

Students can become angry at themselves in much the same manner that they become angry at others. The difference is that instead of someone else breaking a universal commandment, it is they who have broken their own personal commandments.

Anger at oneself can also lead to depression and feelings of guilt. Students believe that they have acted as they should not have and are "worthless" for doing so. According to REBT theory, self-denigration is the cause of most depression. This makes sense when one considers the potential effects of clients telling themselves, "I'm a no good bastard because I. . . ." How could students feel anything but depressed when they are reindoctrinating themselves with such a negative belief throughout the day?

A fifth-grade student was referred to me by her mother, who was concerned about problems Sally was having with her peers. Sally had recently moved into the district and had been having a hard time making friends.

Sally wanted to fit in with her new classmates, which may have been part of the problem. She had a tendency to try too hard to be liked, which produced the opposite effect, driving her classmates away from her.

Her anger came from breaking the rule she held for herself: "I should never act like a fool in front of my classmates." This was an interesting case because not only were there anger difficulties, but Sally was also bothered by anxiety and intermittent depression.

Her anxiety resulted from her belief that, "It would be *horrible, awful*, and *terrible* if I made a fool of myself in front of my classmates." Rational-Emotive Behavior Therapy theory states that anxiety is the result of an individual's exaggeration of an event's "badness." Anxiety will occur when students take unfortunate events such as embarrassing themselves in front of their classmates and turn these events into catastrophes. Sally's depression resulted from her belief, "If I act like a fool it proves what a *worthless, rotten* person I am." Such self-denigrating beliefs will often lead to feelings of guilt and/or depression.

The intervention used to help Sally was Rational-Emotive Imagery (discussed later in this chapter). She was able to generate the rational belief, "Even if I acted like a fool *I could stand it* and *it wouldn't prove I'm a worthless, rotten person.*" I encouraged Sally to practice imagining acting like a fool in front of her classmates and then trying not to feel angry, depressed, or anxious. She stated that walking around the class clucking like a chicken would be about the most foolish thing she could imagine doing. Her homework was to imagine doing just that but using a rational belief to remain calm. She practiced regularly and was much less upset in just a few weeks.

Rational-Emotive Behavior Therapy employs shame-attacking exercises (like walking around clucking like a chicken) as a means of combating certain types of interpersonal anxiety such as excessive shyness. If clients can perform such acts without upsetting themselves, they are well on the way to overcoming interpersonal anxiety. The important point is for the client to be able to perform such behaviors *without* feeling anxious, depressed, or angry.

ANGER AT THE WORLD

This final category of anger is somewhat of a catchall. A certain percentage of children and adolescents will be angry with nearly everyone and everything because their lives are not exactly the way they would like them to be. These students are "difficult customers" (DCs). They often learn irrational beliefs from their parents, who also demonstrate low frustration tolerance. As mentioned previously, there appears to be an increasing number of these students. In their youth they put a strain on the resources of the schools, and as adults they put a strain on society in general. They are usually unhappy because the rest of the world keeps ignoring the dogmatic rules they've handed down.

Andre, a fifteen-year-old sophomore, was in the same support group as Gina. We had worked together outside of group during a couple of previous crises. He was a bright young man, but did not seem to be able to find a group of students to fit in with, so he was alone a great deal of the time. He had a tendency to do demand a lot from the world around him, as demonstrated by the following session excerpt:

> Therapist: So what's up?
> Andre: I'm just feeling sort of rotten.
> T: Rotten as in what?

A: I don't know. Just sort of sick of everything . . . school, teachers, people.

T: Just kind of tired of things.

A: I get sick of all the stupid people around here.

T: You mean people who act stupidly. Remember when we talked about that?

A: Yeah.

T: Tell me what makes you think that.

A: Mrs. Messling is O.K., but Mr. Stahl is such an idiot. He is so stupid. He shouldn't be teaching anyone.

(Author's note—At this point I ignore the two overgeneralizations, that Mr. Stahl *is* an idiot and that he *is* so stupid, because to pursue this would interfere with the flow of the session. Rational-Emotive Behavior Therapy holds that no one *is* an idiot although people at times *act* idiotically. To be an idiot a person would have act like an idiot for every minute from birth until death, which is impossible.)

T: But Andre, all the things that needed to occur for Mr. Stahl to be teaching have occurred, so of course he should be teaching.

A: What? I don't get what you mean.

T: For him to be teaching he would have to hold a teaching certificate, which he does, right?

A: Right.

T: He would have to have been offered a teaching contract, which he was, right?

A: I guess.

T: And he would have to accept the contract and show up here to work, which he did, right?

A: So.

T: So of course he should be teaching, because everything that needed to occur for him to be teaching did occur.

A: My step-dad has been yelling at my mom again.

(Author's note—Notice how Andre moved to an entirely new topic. Rational-Emotive Behavior Therapy practitioners call this "switching the A." It's a technique used by clients when they are being evasive or they aren't interested in the topic being discussed. In this case it is probably the latter, because I do not believe Andre was interested in the logic behind why Mr. Stahl was teaching.)

T: How do you feel about that?

A: Pissed.

T: Angry at your step-dad. What are you thinking about your step-dad yelling to make yourself angry?

A: I'm not really thinking. I just get angry when I hear him yelling. I think, "I wish he'd just leave."

T: That's what you're thinking about him, but what are you thinking about his yelling? Remember a while ago we talked about thoughts causing feelings. You may not be aware of what you are thinking but you are thinking something. Try finishing this sentence, "My step-dad yells at my mom and he. . . ."

A: And he's a jerk.

T: No. What are you saying about him yelling? "He's yelling at my mom and he. . . ."

A: He's got no right to treat her like that.

T: He's still never hit or pushed her or anything, right?

A: No, I don't think he'd do that. He just has his little temper tantrums.

T: You're right, they are temper tantrums. So you say to yourself, "He's got no right to treat her like that." Now I know you don't like him yelling at her, but doesn't he still have the right to yell if he wants to?

A: No.

T: Why doesn't he?

A: He just doesn't. People just can't go around yelling at whoever they want.

T: Think about what I'm saying. It would be good if people treated each other with more respect, but they do have the right to act like jerks, don't they?

A: What do you mean?

T: We all act like jerks sometimes. I do, your step-dad does, your mom does, and I bet you do once in awhile, don't you?

A: Yeah. I guess so.

T: That's what everybody does once in a while. That's our nature. To say, "He's got no right" is like saying, "He's got to be perfect," which he can't be.

A: (Long pause.) I think I see what you mean. It's not really fair for me to think that, but it's not really fair of him to act like such an ass.

T: No, it's not. The other thing is that you can think, "He's got no right," but will that keep him from yelling?

A: Probably not.

T: Probably not. You can make those rules, but he doesn't have to follow them. You're just going to be walking around mad all the time.

Andre and I went on to discuss whether he could change his step-dad's yelling at his mother. He agreed that he probably couldn't. I suggested that we focus on ways he could learn to accept people with all their negative and positive qualities. Whether students like it or not, we live in a world where step-dads yell at mothers and other unpleasant things occur everyday. If it is possible to change some of those unpleasant things, let's do so. If it isn't possible, it would be best to accept the present state of the world and help clients do the same.

THE ABCs OF REBT REVISITED

As mentioned previously, REBT uses a systematic approach to problem clarification and resolution known as the ABCs. This system allows clients and therapist to target irrational beliefs, dispute them, and replace irrational beliefs with rational thoughts.

In the ABC system, *"A"* stands for the *activating event* that occurs immediately before clients become angry. An "A" can be an occurrence of some type, but it can also be a thought or image. For example, it would be entirely possible for individuals to make themselves angry by remembering an injustice that was done to them in the past. In this case the "A" would be the memory of an event and not the actual event itself.

The *"C"* stands for the emotional *consequence* or feeling experienced. In the context of anger, the consequence or feeling will be anger, rage, hate, or bitterness.

The "C" can also be behavioral, meaning what clients "do" as the result of the "A." A client can withdraw from a situation, and the "C" in that case would be appropriately labeled withdrawal.

As has been illustrated, most people believe that "A" causes "C" (e.g., getting egg salad rather than peanut butter causes anger), which is an erroneous belief. There is a middle part ("B") between "A" and "C" that actually causes anger. *"B"* stands for *belief* or what an individual tells himself or herself about the activating event at point "A."

Beliefs can generally be divided into two broad categories: *rational beliefs* (RB) and *irrational beliefs* (IB). Two general rules of thumb are particularly useful in determining whether a belief is rational or irrational. Rational beliefs are supported by *empirical evidence* and produce *moderate emotional responses;* Irrational beliefs have no empirical support and produce extreme emotional responses. An example may help clarify this point.

A senior in high school, Amy, is angry at her father because he won't allow her to go to a concert in Milwaukee. Her father says it's not appropriate to go to a concert on a school night. To illustrate how different thoughts produce different feelings, this example uses both rational and irrational thoughts at point "B."

Irrational Belief

A—Amy's father will not allow her to go to the concert.

At point "B" Amy believes the following: "He *has no right* to keep me home when all my friends get to go. He *shouldn't* be so overprotective."

At point "C" Amy feels angry.

Rational Belief

A—Amy's father will not allow her to go to the concert.

This time Amy tells herself this rational thought at point "B": "I *don't like it* when he won't let me go places. He's probably overprotective because he loves me. He *does* have the right to make the rules in the house, but I don't have to like them."

Such a thought leads to upset feelings, but rather than being extremely angry or enraged, Amy feels only irritation at point "C."

Notice that the "A" (activating event) stayed the same. However, the "C" (consequence or feeling) changed when the "B" was different. This lends more support to the idea that "As" do not cause "Cs." If events caused feelings, how could the same event (not going to the concert) produce two different emotions (anger and irritation)?

Some critics of REBT mistakenly believe that REBT is preaching a Pollyanna approach to problems ("Don't worry, be happy"). This criticism is incorrect but is heard fairly often by REBT practitioners.

Rational-Emotive Behavior Therapy is not stating that Amy would enjoy being refused permission to go to the concert by her father. The practitioner would not expect Amy to be happy about this event. It would be appropriate (and natural) to be moderately upset in such a situation. To expect an adolescent to "like" being denied permission to go on a social outing with friends is ridiculous.

Although Amy may not like the outcome, this does not mean her father does not have the right to act as he acted (refusing to give her permission to go to the concert). It would not make sense to become enraged by demanding that her father act differently than he had acted. *He should have acted exactly as he acted because that is how he acted.* To think otherwise is a failure to accept reality. It is always irrational to demand that other people act in a manner other than the way they acted. Amy doesn't control her father's behavior, and if he decides to set limits such as curfews, that's what he is going to do no matter how objectionable it may be to Amy. Nothing will be accomplished by *demanding* he act differently. It certainly will not force her father to change. People are fallible, error-prone beings, and to demand they be otherwise is silly. It is analogous to asking someone to be better at being who they are, a request they obviously will not meet.

Once the irrational belief at point "B" is clearly defined, it is time to move on to "D," which stands for *disputation.* This is the point at which the counselor disputes and/or debates with clients about their irrational beliefs at point "B." There are numerous disputation techniques, which are examined later in this chapter, but a starting point and excellent initial question is, "Where's the proof for that belief?"

Therapist: Amy, here at point "B" you agree that you are saying to yourself, "He *has no right* to keep me home when all my friends get to go. He *shouldn't* be so overprotective." Is that right?

Amy: Yes.

T: So you believe your father has no right to make those decisions about you and your curfew?

A: I do everything he asks me to do. I do good in school. I love Britney Spears and I have to go to that concert.

T: Remember how we talked about the differences between rational and irrational beliefs?

A: (Nods head in agreement.)

T: Explain what you remember to me.

(Author's note—Asking clients to explain a concept is an excellent way to assess whether they were listening. Often they will appear to understand but do not clearly comprehend an idea.)

A: A rational belief is like a true idea. An irrational belief isn't true.

T: What about proof? Can you remember that?

A: Oh, yeah. We can prove a rational belief. Like with the diet pill. . . . Give the pill to 100 people and if they lose weight, they've proven it works.

T: Good. Now let's get back to your belief about your father. Can you prove that he has no right to keep you from that concert?

A: Yes! (quite emphatically)

T: O.K. Prove it to me.

A: I hate it when he's so overprotective.

T: I didn't ask you whether you like it or not. I know you don't like it. I don't think anyone would. I asked if you could prove that he has no right to say it.

A: He doesn't have the right. It's my life. I'm on the honor role every semester. I just want this one thing and he can't say "no" just like that. He didn't even think about it.

T: Then prove that to me. You haven't proven it to me yet.

A: What do you mean, "Prove it?"

T: You have a theory that your father has no right to say you can't go. I want you to show me evidence that your theory is true.

A: (Long pause.) I can't show you evidence.

T: Then is your belief rational or irrational?

A: Irrational, I guess.

(Author's note—At this point Amy agrees that her belief is irrational, but it doesn't appear that she really believes that to be true. I'm convinced she still believes her father has no right to keep her from going. My hunch is she still believes he shouldn't be so overprotective. More disputing had better be done to convince Amy that her idea doesn't make sense.)

T: Do you know the 1st Amendment?

A: I think so.

T: It has to do with freedom of . . . what?

A: Freedom of speech.

T: Right. What that means is that people have the constitutional right to say what they want. Your belief that your father can't say, "You're not going to that concert on a school night," is saying he doesn't have that right. Your idea is *unconstitutional*! It's *un-American*!

A: (Laughs.)

T: Now, who has more power, the Constitution or Amy?

A: The Constitution.

T: Probably right. Because the name of this country isn't the United States of Amy, is it? But I want to make sure you understand I'm not saying you have to like missing the concert.

A: I know what you mean.

T: But he does have the right to do what you don't like.

A: I guess you're right.

The next step in the ABC analysis is to produce a rational belief to replace the irrational belief at point "B." This can usually be done by simply changing a word or two in the irrational belief, thereby making it rational. For example:

Irrational belief: "He *has no right* to keep me home when all my friends get to go. He *shouldn't* be so overprotective." This IB can be changed to an RB by simply substituting the word "the" for "no."

Rational belief: "He *does* have the right to keep me home when all my friends get to go." It is usually helpful to add a modifier at the end of the newly created RB. ("He does have the right to keep me home BUT I DON'T HAVE TO LIKE IT.")

The final step is *"E,"* which stands for the new *effect* produced by substituting an RB for an IB. If the RB, "He has the right to talk to me that way but I don't have to like it" is used to replace the IB, "He has NO right. . . ," it would most likely produce a moderate emotional response. Instead of feeling enraged or extremely angry as Amy felt at point "C," she would probably feel less angry or only irritated. There is a big difference between irritation, which is an appropriate response to disappointment, and anger, which will do nothing to help her survive, reach her goals, or allow her to experience the emotions she wants to experience.

Some people will think, "Why doesn't this child have the right to be angry that her father is keeping her from going to a concert? She makes a good argument that her grades are good and it's only for one night."

The child or adolescent does have the right to be angry, because people have the right to think and feel whatever they want. People can believe that others have to treat them fairly or that the world shouldn't be such a cruel place. However, such thinking does nothing to help them cope with the day-to-day difficulties they will run into. Believing that others do not have the right to act the way they have acted is just plain wrong. Others have the right to do what they want, and no amount of demanding will take that right away. It will do nothing but cause more anger in similar situations in the future.

Helping a child be less angry is not taking away a defense. A much better defense is to arm the child with the power to eliminate negative emotions. When students learn skills so that other people can no longer upset them, that is real power! In this day and age, what better defense could a child or adolescent possess?

Anger, in the above scenario, could lead to dangerous behavior such as Amy yelling at her father and provoking a much bigger problem. By not becoming angry, a child is less likely to make such unwise decisions.

Early on in the therapeutic process, clients have a difficult time changing IBs into RBs. Therapists have to provide assistance to clients until they become proficient at challenging and changing beliefs by themselves. This can be problematic in that counselors are using their words to produce rational beliefs rather than having clients use their own vocabulary. It is always best to allow children and adolescents to spontaneously produce their own RBs. One of the best techniques to help clients do this is Rational-Emotive Imagery (REI).

RATIONAL-EMOTIVE IMAGERY

Rational-emotive imagery technique has numerous applications and has been found to be beneficial in helping clients change irrational beliefs into rational beliefs. It is discussed here as a means of assisting clients in the production of their own rational thoughts.

REI is actually a mild form of hypnosis, but it may be unwise to share this information with kids. There is a common misconception that individuals can be made to do things against their will while under hypnosis. It's best to simply tell children that you have an idea for a game they might like. Almost all children enjoy playing games, and they usually will be more than willing to play this new game. With older students (middle and high school) it is usually possible to skip this explanation altogether.

Start by telling clients that you want them to get as relaxed as possible, sitting with both feet on the floor. It usually works best to have students place their hands in their laps. Following is an example of how I typically use REI.

Kenny was a student who was very "needy." He would become very upset even when little things didn't go his way. In this example he was angry because he had asked a friend to let him cut in line and the friend had refused.

Therapist: Kenny, I want you to listen very closely to what I say. I want you to only be aware of my voice and focus on what I say.

Close your eyes and take a deep breath. As you breathe out, notice that you are becoming more relaxed. Each time you breathe out you are getting more relaxed and more focused on my voice. The only thing you are aware of is my voice.

Imagine you are back in the lunch room and David wouldn't let you cut into the line and you made yourself angry. Imagine everything about the lunch room. Smell the food. Hear the sounds of the people talking. See everything around you in the lunch room. Now picture in your mind David telling you that he won't let you cut in line. Feel all the anger you felt then. Go ahead and make yourself angry again. When you get good and angry, wiggle your finger to let me know you're there.

(Author's note—It's a good idea to look for behavioral signs confirming that the client is actually angry, such as a clenched jaw or flared nostrils.)

Stay good and angry. Keep imagining that you are right there in the lunch room.

(Author's note—Allow the child to stay in this angered state for approximately twenty to forty seconds. Remind him or her to remain in the situation and to remain angry.)

Now I want you to calm yourself down. Stay in the lunch room in your mind, but try to calm down. Pretend David has just told you that you can't cut in line, but instead of being angry, try to remain calm. Keep working at it until you can calm yourself down. When you can make yourself calm, wiggle your finger again.

Usually clients can reach a state of relative calm within a short time. The first question to ask is, *"What did you say to yourself to calm yourself down?"* If they were able to calm themselves, they were most likely thinking a rational thought. The only other way to distinguish the anger would be for them to mentally leave the situation (i.e., no longer visualizing the lunch room or changing the situation in some way). This usually doesn't happen, but if it does, try the exercise over, encouraging the client to keep imagining the scene but working to calm down.

Clients will sometimes ask, "Am I doing this right?" If they were able to calm themselves down, they were doing the procedure correctly. As the old saying goes, the proof of the pudding is in the eating. If they can imagine the situation and not be angry, they are thinking rationally.

The RB that clients produce can then be recorded for use in homework assignments. A typical RB that might have been produced from the above scenario would be, "David doesn't have to let me cut in line. I can wait with the rest of the students."

The real advantage of using this technique is that the RB comes from within rather than from the counselor. Give this technique a try; it is this simple and it does work.

ANGER DISPUTATIONS AND INTERVENTIONS

Rational-Emotive Behavior Therapy uses cognitive, behavioral, and emotive techniques to help students see the errors in their thinking. Following is a discussion of disputations and interventions to use with clients who have anger problems. Many of these techniques have been discussed previously in this book but are highlighted again in this section.

Disputations are essential in the practice of REBT because it is through the disputation process that clients are helped to the realization that what they have been telling themselves does not make sense. It is important to know as many disputation techniques as possible, because some arguments work well with some clients and not as well with others. The more ammunition in your arsenal of arguments, the better. If you think of yourself as a carpenter, these arguments are your tools.

The more tools you have and the more talented you are at using those tools, the better your chances of being successful in building your house.

It is also helpful to gather biographical information about the student before the disputation process begins. Information regarding clients' hobbies and interests is useful during disputations. For example, if clients have an interest in athletics, use an example that incorporates sporting concepts during the disputation. Following is an example of personal data used in disputation with a client who is discouraged because he is not having success learning how to control his anger:

> Therapist: So you had a bad day yesterday in Mr. Lilla's class?
>
> Gary: Yes, I was trying to get my test done and I ran out of time. When he said I had to hand it in I wasn't finished and I told him I wanted to work on it some more. He said I couldn't and I slammed my desk down. That got me an office referral. I don't think I'm ever going to get this stuff.
>
> T: Do you think everything has to come easy? You told me your favorite team is the Dallas Cowboys, right?
>
> G: Yes.
>
> T: They used to be the worst team in football. They lost fifteen of sixteen games a few years ago but they never gave up. What do you think they did to improve as players?
>
> G: Tried harder?
>
> T: That's right. They decided if what they were doing wasn't good enough, they had better figure out a way to get it to work. And that's what we've got to do.

Cognitive Techniques

The goal of most cognitive techniques is to get students to question the logic of their beliefs (Walen, DiGiuseppe, and Wessler, 1980). Most schools of psychotherapy discourage "why" questions, but such questions can be used effectively in REBT.

All educators have had to deal with students who are upset because they have been called a name. Following is a short segment demonstrating how the REBT approach can be used to encourage students to rethink name calling.

Lee Ann: She can't say I'm a dweeb!
Therapist: Why not?
L: She just can't.
T: Why?
L: It's not very nice.
T: Why can't she act that way, though? I agree it's not very nice, but why can't she be "not nice?"
L: Because I don't like it.
T: But why do you have to like it?

One of the most difficult things for people to accept is that *people have the right to be wrong*. Most people are raised to believe that because most individuals would agree that certain behaviors are objectionable, humans *must not* behave in that way. Most would agree that it would be nice if people didn't call other people "dweebs." This does not mean they *must* not. This point has been belabored, but I promise you that it will be difficult for many clients and adults to accept. Be especially sensitive to the difficulty of helping clients accept this reality.

Another excellent cognitive disputation involves helping clients see that by getting angry at someone, they are letting that individual control them. Since the individual they are angered at has already carried out a perceived misdeed against them, it is doubly foolish to now let this person control how they feel. By getting angry, clients are letting this other individual win again. This disputation is a way of letting clients use their anger in a constructive manner. Because they are already upset with the offending party, the therapist can motivate them to give up their anger:

Therapist: So let me see if I understand, Mike copied your homework and you're mad at him?
Dan: Yeah.
T: Wow, Mike is getting to win twice.
D: What do you mean "win twice?"
T: Well, not only did he get to copy your homework but now he's controlling how you feel. He's winning twice.
D: I've never thought of it that way.
T: If I were you I wouldn't want Mike to be able to control how I feel. He already got your homework, now he's ruining your day.

The Use of Humor

Humor and exaggeration can be used to show clients they are thinking in an irrational manner. Humor can also be used to help establish rapport with clients.

Rational-Emotive Behavior Therapy does not view the therapeutic relationship as all-important, as many client-centered therapies do, but establishing a strong relationship with clients has several advantages. Clients who respect and genuinely like their therapists are more likely to practice between sessions. They also appear to trust their therapists more and are willing to give this new type of thinking a chance.

The following excerpt from a session is a good illustration of the REBT concept that most emotional problems come from "demandingness" of some form or other. In this case the client was demanding that a friend sit with him at lunch:

> Therapist: So you believe that Paula has to eat lunch with you every-day or you are going to be mad.
> Mitch: I don't think that's too much to ask.
> T: But why stop there? Why not demand that she do only what you want twenty-four hours a day? And why not demand that you win the lottery? Why not demand that you win every lottery? Why not demand that you win the lottery without having to buy a ticket?

By exaggerating the situation to such a ridiculous extreme, it is hoped that clients will see it is unwise to demand anything that they don't have control over.

The Search for Control Technique

When clients state, "She made me so mad," try looking around on the floor as if you had lost something. When they ask what you're looking for say, "Your control."

> Steve: Are you looking for something?
> Therapist: Yes, your control.
> S: My control?
> T: Somehow you've lost your control over your feelings. We all have

the ability to control how we feel, but somehow you've lost yours. How else could someone make you angry?

You can use the same technique with students who blame their difficulties on their "bad temper." It is not uncommon for students to use this reasoning as an excuse so they do not have to accept responsibility for their behavior. You'll hear students say things like, "I've had a bad temper all my life," or "I've got a bad temper just like everyone in my family." Students speak of a "temper" as if it is something they have no control over.

> Steve: Are you looking for something?
> Therapist: Yes, my bad temper.
> S: Your temper?
> T: I lost it about the time I stopped demanding the world treat me fairly.

Paradoxical Intention

The use of paradoxical intention may be beneficial with some clients who do not respond to other disputations. The idea behind this intervention is to persuade the student to behave paradoxically regarding the agreed-upon goals of treatment. For example, if a student is extremely angry at a classmate, try to convince the client to act especially nice toward his or her agitator. Ellis (1977b) states that by deliberately behaving in a paradoxical manner, the client may feel less angry. The client's appropriate behavior could serve as a model for others to follow. The client's behaving in this paradoxical manner could also encourage the offending party to examine his or her behavior and act more appropriately in the future.

Other techniques that incorporate paradoxical features can be beneficial. With a student who has anger problems the therapist might suggest, "Try to be as angry as you can be all day long." Trying to stay angry all day is difficult because it requires a lot of energy. Students will literally exhaust themselves trying to remain upset. Telling students to stay angry appears to have the opposite effect, and they actually experience less anger.

A variation of this approach is to give the client permission to be angry, but only for short periods of time. ("Try to be angry only between 8:00 and 8:15 each morning.") If students are able to follow these directions, the amount of time they spend feeling upset is significantly reduced. It is better to have a student very angry for a short period of time than "simmering" all day long. What often happens is that 8:15 arrives and the student hasn't been angry at all. Of course it is better to give students the skills to challenge their anger-producing philosophies, which paradoxical intention does not do.

Cognitive Distraction

Another technique, reserved primarily for resistant clients, is cognitive distraction. This technique also has the limitation of not changing students' philosophical stance that things must go the way they want. As the name implies, this technique is merely a distraction designed to keep the client from lapsing into a rage state.

To use this technique effectively, it is best to first teach clients deep relaxation techniques. Most children can learn these techniques and benefit from having such skills. However, many clients are hesitant to use them. Also, students often are not in surroundings that are conducive to deep muscle relaxation.

Another distraction technique, which does not require deep muscle relaxation and can be used anywhere, involves having clients think of either the funniest or happiest memory they have. The memory is best if it can produce an instantaneous smile or laugh.

Instruct clients that when they are starting to feel themselves becoming angry they are to immediately shut their eyes and picture their pre-selected scene. Some clients are quite successful with this technique. It is also an excellent technique to help clients deal with anxiety. It is nearly impossible to be angry or anxious when you are picturing a very funny event from the past.

Behavioral Techniques

Reinforcement

Rational-Emotive Behavior Therapy encourages the use of standard behavioral techniques as a means of changing irrational beliefs. The most effective and commonly used behavioral intervention is reinforcement.

Reinforcement can be used in a number of different ways in the course of therapy. Students can receive reinforcement when they have completed their therapeutic homework assignments. Parents can be enlisted to monitor homework completion and administer the reinforcement. It is not difficult to explain to parents the activities clients are to practice. Some type of behavioral contract can be arranged regarding what reinforcement clients can earn for completing the agreed-upon assignment. This type of program has the advantage of keeping the parents involved and aware of clients' treatment and progress.

Reinforcement can also be used as a means of encouraging clients to stay in control of their behavior. The above-mentioned contract can include a section specifying the rewards clients can earn if they lose their tempers fewer than three times a week, for example. Most clients can identify special treats or privileges they will work toward. Following is a list of commonly used reinforcers that children and adolescents seem to enjoy:

- phone privileges
- video rental
- curfew extension
- use of car
- pizza
- soft drink
- reduced chores
- later bedtime
- candy
- a special toy
- Nintendo rental
- special trip
- camping
- friend staying over
- cassette tape
- make-up
- special meal

- going to movies
- parent time
- playing outside
- new T-shirt
- no baby-sitting
- money
- not making bed

Parents and clients will have to work out an agreement that includes reinforcers specific to their own situation.

The disadvantage of such a system is that clients have to be responsible for monitoring their own anger episodes. The parents are only able to monitor the students' behavior when they are around them, which is a relatively small percentage of the time.

Rubber Band Technique

A technique that is similar to cognitive distraction is the rubber band technique. Clients wear a rubber band around their wrists. When they feel themselves becoming angry, they are to snap themselves with the rubber band. The snapping of the rubber band is a reminder to immediately practice their rational beliefs.

This technique can also be used when clients hear themselves thinking "shoulds," "musts," "have tos," and "ought tos." When they identify such commandments they are to snap themselves and replace these irrational beliefs with rational thoughts.

The snapping is a mildly aversive stimulus, but don't think of this technique as punishment. The snapping is more helpful as a reminder to use rational coping statements for clients who have a hard time remembering to change those irrational voices to rational thoughts.

Planned Avoidance

Sometimes discretion is the better part of valor. Some students with anger problems experience difficulties in very specific situations or only with certain people. For example, it is not uncommon for students to have feuds with certain classmates or to have difficulties in certain settings, such as after lunch free time. It may be appropriate to help clients think about managing the amount of time they spend in these situations or with these people.

Counselors may have to help clients use some common sense. Maybe they can eat lunch at a different table so they aren't always exposed to people they become angry with, or maybe they should associate with different people during free time after lunch. Learning to problem solve is a very important skill that students will use for the rest of their lives.

Emotive Techniques

Rational-Emotive Imagery

Rational-Emotive Imagery is my disputation of choice with angry clients. It was described previously in this chapter and is only briefly summarized here.

Have clients picture the scenario in which they angered themselves. Encourage them to become angry but, after a few moments of being angry, they are to calm themselves down. They are to continue to imagine the scene but attempt to talk to themselves in a rational manner so that they will be only irritated and not enraged.

Pragmatic Disputes

Dryden (1990) recommends the use of pragmatic disputes, which can be very effective with difficult clients. This technique is designed to vividly point out the consequences of clinging to irrational beliefs.

As has been discussed, the result of irrational thinking is usually needless emotional suffering. In the case of anger, the irrational demand that things *should* go the way clients would like them to causes a great deal of time to be spent being upset. Pragmatic disputes try to make this crystal clear to clients.

Ellis (1962; 1985) often says things such as, "If you continue to believe that the world must treat you fairly, you'll probably suffer for the rest of your life." When clients tell Ellis they cannot change their

beliefs, he points out the logical consequences of retaining their irrational beliefs by emphatically stating, "So suffer!"

A slight variation to this theme that I have found to be very effective
is to explain to clients that they have every right to believe that others
must do what they would like. *They also have the right to all the misery
their hearts can bear.* I then ask, "Have you ever seen a news story
that says, 'There was a shortage of misery in the world today'?" When
the client says "no" I explain, "Then you have every right to keep on
believing that others must treat you fairly and feeling miserable
because of that belief."

Forceful Dialogue

With this disputation, clients are encouraged to forcefully argue with
themselves regarding their irrational beliefs. This technique resembles
a conversation except that there is only one person talking. The client
is speaking in both the rational and irrational voices:

> Irrational: Teachers have to treat me fairly.
> *Rational: It would be nice if teachers treated me fairly but there isn't
> any evidence that they have to do so.*
> Irrational: But they should be fair.
> *Rational: There is not one reason why they should act any other way
> than the way they acted.*
> Irrational: The world has to be a better place to live. There are too
> many bad things.
> *Rational: It is true that there are many bad things, but how many is
> too many? Too many means different things to different people. Don't
> forget that there are a lot of enjoyable things also. The world is not a
> good or bad place. It is a place where things happen and people decide
> if these things are good or bad.*

Full Acceptance

The intervention of full acceptance is actually a disputation but may
not appear to be. Therapists fully accept clients with all of their positive
and negative traits. The fact that clients have problem areas in their
lives does not make them any less valuable or less human. By demon-

strating to clients that their therapist accepts them (and their anger problems), it is hoped that they will be able to accept themselves.

One of the irrational ideas that causes the most suffering is that people can be given a global rating according to the "goodness" of their actions. To students, this often means that to feel good about themselves, they have to act correctly 100 percent of the time. If they are able to give up this idea, they will spend less time trying to earn their worth and have more time and energy to concentrate on overcoming their anger problems.

It is not uncommon to see students who originally were referred for an anger problem develop an additional problem related to their difficulties in overcoming their original problem. For example, students who are having a hard time overcoming an anger problem can become depressed by their lack of success. Some have referred to this phenomenon as *symptom stress,* when the anger at "C" becomes the "A" in depression:

A—Student is grounded for breaking curfew.

B—"My parents *shouldn't* be so strict. I *ought to* be able to stay out later like my friends."

C—Anger.

The anger at point "C" now becomes a triggering event at point "A," which leads to self-denigration.

A—Student becomes angry over being grounded.

B—"There I go again making myself angry. *I can't do anything right! I am so worthless.* I'll never learn how to keep myself from getting angry.

C—Depression.

When students are taught to fully accept themselves along with their difficulties, they will be much less likely to spin into such a negative spiral.

Emotional Training

Ramsey (1974) described a technique he called *emotional training* that can be effective when students are angry with others. Ask students to recall pleasant experiences they have had with the individual with whom they now feel angry. The students are to imagine all the pleasant exchanges they have had with this individual until the warm, happy feelings overpower the angry, hostile feelings.

This intervention can be given as homework and may be effective at keeping students from "stewing" over negative feelings. In effect, this is reversing the process whereby intensely negative feelings are created. Rather than students harping on feelings of anger and hatred, they are focusing on pleasant memories.

Rational Role Reversal

This technique has a definite cognitive component, but it is categorized here as an emotive disputation because it helps deepen clients' conviction to rational thinking. There is some interesting research on the phenomenon of cognitive dissonance to support the concept behind Rational Role Reversal (RRR).

Cognitive dissonance exists when an individual's beliefs and behavior are not in congruence. If people believe stealing is immoral and then steal, there is a lack of consistency between their beliefs and behavior. Individuals in a state of dissonance will attempt to somehow regain consistency between their beliefs and behaviors. To do this, clients can either change their behavior or change their belief system. In the theft example, clients could return what was stolen or change their beliefs so that stealing is acceptable under some circumstances.

Rational Role Reversal involves having clients and therapists switch roles. Therapists tell clients what made them angry, and the clients' job is to dispute the irrational ideas put forth by their therapists. This technique is usually fun for both clients and therapists, but it also provides therapists with valuable information regarding which ideas clients have or have not fully comprehended. Pay particular attention to the disputations the clients use (while acting as the therapist) because these are the arguments that have made the biggest impression on them.

It is important to realize that clients can have an intellectual understanding of concepts but may not have an emotional understanding or commitment. Clients can recite the logic of the argument but don't truly believe the disputation has merit. For lasting change to occur, clients have to adopt these new philosophies wholeheartedly.

Assertiveness Training

Helping students learn to stand up for themselves is included here as an intervention because often anger is used to cover feelings of embarrassment or humiliation. When students are able to stand up for themselves in an appropriate manner they are less likely to be taken advantage of and will experience fewer situations in which they anger themselves.

One of the most effective means of teaching students to be more assertive is through role play or behavioral rehearsal. Students are encouraged to give examples of situations in which they find it difficult to stand up for themselves. Once they have given the therapist or group a couple of examples, they can be given the opportunity to practice being assertive. The therapist or group can give clients feedback on their performance and they can role play the situation again. Clients can also practice alone in front of a mirror.

If this assignment is especially difficult for some clients, it might be a good idea to examine the irrational beliefs causing them difficulties and keeping them from being more assertive. It has been my experience that the core IB associated with a lack of assertiveness usually contains a rational and irrational segment. The student usually believes, "If I told them what I really thought they may not like me," which is rational. Often when people tell others they don't agree with them or they don't appreciate how they were just treated, the assertive individual is criticized or scorned. The irrational belief associated with this difficulty is usually, "And if they didn't like me, that would be *horrible* or prove what a *rotten person* I am." This irrational belief can be disputed and, hopefully, the student will come to realize that if others did not like him or her, it would not be a catastrophe, merely an inconvenience. It certainly would not prove he or she is "rotten" because another person's opinion has no real power.

Rational Story Telling Technique

As mentioned previously, the cognitive limitations of younger children must be taken into consideration if counseling is going to be effective at helping them control their anger. Younger clients aren't abstract thinkers, and many of the more commonly employed disputations rely on abstract thought. The rational story telling technique is a simple and straightforward intervention that can be effective with younger children.

This technique involves having a child and therapist tell each other stories. The two rules are 1) that the child always goes first and 2) that the story has to be made up and can't come from a movie or television program.

The therapist listens to the story and looks for the irrational ideas contained within the tale. The therapist then tells his or her story, making it similar to the child's but replacing the irrational ideas with rational thoughts.

The following story was told to me by a client referred to me by his mother. She explained that Nick had numerous temper tantrums, which he also occasionally experienced at school. He was in second grade at the time of this session.

> Nick: Once upon a time there was a big goat that lived in a forest. He liked to play with the other goats but they didn't want to play with him. He got mad and butted the other goats with his horns but they still wouldn't play with him so he yelled and kicked and cried. The end.

Obviously, the goat in the story was Nick. I told Nick the following story.

> My story is also about a big goat that lived in a forest. He also had problems making friends with other goats. Then one day he realized getting mad and butting the other goats wouldn't make the other goats like him. He also realized yelling and crying wouldn't make the other goats want to play with him.
>
> Instead he decided to nicely ask the other goats if he could join them in their game. If they said "no" he knew he didn't have to get mad. He could always play with other goats or by himself. It took a while but the other goats found out that the big goat was fun to play with. They used to not like the way he butted them but he didn't do that anymore. The goat was happy that he now had more friends to play with.

Not all stories are as perfectly lined up with the presenting problem of anger. No matter what the child's story is about, the therapist can always incorporate a message that encourages the client to remain in control of his or her anger.

Time Projection

When students are angry, they often do not realize that problems have a way of diminishing over time. Very few events have a permanent impact on students' lives. The purpose of time projection is to get the students to imagine the world *after* the problem has become less important.

If an adolescent is extremely angry about a situation, encourage the student to imagine a month, two months, or a year in the future. Ask, "Do you think the problem you're having with your math teacher is going to be on your mind two years from now?" It is not uncommon for a student to even chuckle at such a suggestion. Chances are the student won't even remember the situation by then, and therefore it is not worth the continual emotional upset he or she is currently experiencing. By getting the client to realize that this problem is a time-limited inconvenience, he or she is often able to obtain a better perspective.

Anger Charting

Another technique to help students with anger problems involves keeping a chart of times when they "explode." A simple chart with the days of the week is all that is needed. Students are instructed to record answers to the following questions:

- Where were you when you got angry?
- Who else was present?
- Describe the situation (what happened?).
- On a scale from 1 to 100, how angry were you?

This information can help the client and counselor look for trends in the anger episodes. Does the student have problems on Mondays or in certain classes? The data collected can help with the formulation of a practical plan and also can make the client aware of his or her tendencies.

Role Playing

As mentioned previously, practicing new ways of thinking and behaving are very important in achieving success. Role playing can help considerably in this regard.

There are many different ways to use role playing, but one that I like relates to anger charting and planned avoidance. Once information has been gathered (through anger charting) a role play can be designed around the situations that often lead to anger episodes. The counselor or other group members reenact the situation with the client. The first step is for the client to "walk through" the situation, making his or her cognitions known by speaking his or her thoughts. These thoughts can then be analyzed after the role play to determine whether the beliefs are helpful (rational, self-calming) or harmful (irrational, self-agitating). It is best to let the client try to adopt his or her own self-calming thoughts, but if all else fails, the counselor should make suggestions (e.g., "How would you feel if you thought . . . ?"). Don't forget to plan what the client can do *behaviorally* as well. For example, would it be wise to move away from the situation and avoid direct eye contact?

CONCLUSION

Anger often occurs when others block a client's goal, attack a client's values, threaten a client, or break a client's rules. Anger can also be directed inward toward the self or outward at the world in general.

The ABCs is a system of problem clarification and resolution:

A—Activating event (what happened)
B—Belief (what we thing about the activating event)
C—Consequence (what we feel or do)
D—Disputation (how we argue with ourselves about the irrational beliefs)
E—New effect (how we feel with our new rational philosophy)

Disputations are cognitive, behavioral, or emotive:

Cognitive
• Why?
• The use of humor

- Search for control
- Paradoxical intention
- Cognitive distraction

Behavioral
- Reinforcement
- Rubber band technique
- Planned avoidance

Emotive
- Rational-Emotive Imagery
- Pragmatic disputes
- Forceful dialogue
- Full acceptance
- Emotional training
- Rational Role Reversal
- Assertiveness training
- Rational story telling technique
- Time projection
- Anger charting
- Role playing

CHAPTER 8

Depression, Anger, and Aggression

It is easy to overlook depression as a causative factor in the misbehavior of angry and aggressive students. Teachers, parents, and mental health professionals can become fixated on the student's *behavior* rather than on the *cause* of the conduct. However, it is essential that practitioners first learn what is driving the behavior prior to treatment. If depression is the primary cause for the misbehavior, it only makes sense to treat the depression rather than focusing solely on the angry outbursts or noncompliance with teacher requests. Otherwise the primary source of the problem will be left untreated.

A majority of children and adolescents who have difficulties with anger could be described as *externalizers,* which explains the commonly used term "acting out." However, there are thousands of anger-prone students who are also suffering from an *internalizing* disorder, namely depression. A review of literature on this topic found that between 21 and 83 percent of children diagnosed with oppositional defiant disorder or conduct disorder were also suffering from a depressive disorder (Angold and Costello, 1993). Although there is considerable variation in the rates of depression cited among the various studies, one thing is clear: Even at the low end of the spectrum (i.e., 21 percent), there are still thousands of children and adolescents battling depression, many with little or no support.

Following is a list of characteristics thought to be associated with depression:

- feelings of sadness, hopelessness, and worthlessness
- irritability

- references to suicide (e.g., "I'd be better off dead."; "Nobody would care if I wasn't around.")
- loss of energy
- change in sleep patterns, either waking up early and not being able to get back to sleep or wanting to sleep all the time
- significant change in weight
- giving away prized possessions
- interest in death (e.g., reading books on death)
- decrease in physical activity
- uncontrollable crying
- excessive guilt
- loss of interest in activities that were previously enjoyed

It is important to note that a significant number of children with anger problems do not present many of the classic symptoms mentioned above. They may not appear to feel sad or worthless, which is why they are often misdiagnosed or go completely undiagnosed. They often come across as simply noncompliant. That's why depression in angry and aggressive students is so often missed by counselors.

PREVALENCE OF DEPRESSION

Depression in children and adolescents is a significant problem, with thousands of students being effected. Petersen et al. (1993) found that 20–35 percent of adolescent boys and 25–40 percent of girls reported having depressed moods, and Reynolds (1992) found that 4–12 percent were clinically depressed. Wilde (1994) conducted a study using eighty high school students who were given the Beck Depression Inventory (BDI). Of these eighty randomly selected high school students, 25 percent were found to be at least mildly depressed. Fava et al. (1993) reported that of the 44 percent of outpatients who met the diagnostic criteria (DSM-III-R) for major depression, 21 percent also reported the presence of anger attacks.

DEPRESSION AND ANGER

The most common behavioral manifestation of depression in some children is anger and irritability. These students cover or deny their feelings of worthlessness with rage and often aggressively act out their anger. Aggressive expression of anger and anger level in general have been found to be predictors of depression in ten- and eleven-year-old boys (Blumberg and Izard, 1985). At school they can often be found in the principal's office, because they are constantly in some sort of trouble due to fights or difficulties getting along with teachers and peers. Research by Kashani et al. (1995) suggested that depressed children are less able to control their angry feelings in a thoughtful, nonimpulsive manner.

There is another substrate of depressed children who may not even exhibit the above mentioned unmodulated hostility. It's not that these children aren't angry, it's just that they aren't as comfortable expressing their anger and frustration. They exhibit other behaviors that are negative predictors of adjustment, such as

- cruelty to animals,
- pyromania, and
- encopresis (soiling oneself).

This small cluster of behaviors is also indicative of other serious disorders, but be aware that many of these children are also depressed.

THE COGNITIVE ETIOLOGY OF DEPRESSION

The cognitive therapist Aaron Beck postulated three primary beliefs that lead to depression. Beck and Shaw (1977) referred to these beliefs as the "cognitive triad."

1. Negative View of the Self

Typical self-talk from depressed individuals that represents this philosophy often includes statements such as:

"I am no damn good and I never will amount to anything."
"I deserve the rotten treatment I get."
"No matter what I do, I will fail."

"I can't do anything right."

"Nobody could love me because I am worthless."

There is another interesting phenomenon associated with children who suffer from these types of beliefs. They have a tendency to blame themselves excessively and take responsibility for failures that were not necessarily their fault. The team they play on loses, so these children think, "It's probably my fault we lost because I was on the team. If I had only hit a home run every time up to bat, we might have won."

When these children do succeed, they often feel they deserve none of the credit. Depressed children and adolescents often will not accept recognition for their hard work and prefer to explain the outcome as "luck." This type of thinking is emotional double jeopardy. If they fail a test, they believe, "This proves how dumb I am." If they receive a high score, they think, "Boy, was I ever lucky."

2. Negative View of the World

Not only do depressed children feel *they* are hopeless, many feel the *world* is a hopeless place as well. They seem to think the problems of the world are beyond repair:

"What is the point of going on?"

"You have to watch your back, because people are out to take advantage of you."

"Any day now, the world is going to end. It can't go on like this."

3. Negative View of the Future

Many depressed children believe that the unfortunate circumstances they are currently experiencing will continue forever. Many look into the future and see nothing but darkness and more difficulties:

"There is no way out."

"I'll never get over this."

"I can't change the horrible things that have happened to me in the past so I'm doomed forever."

"Life sucks now and will always suck."

It is important to realize that there are many corollaries from the three core irrational beliefs contained in Beck's cognitive triad. Numerous variations exist, but all seem to have originated from one of these three ideas about the self, the world, and the future. The sample messages given above are just a few of the irrational beliefs that cluster around these core cognitions leading to depression.

ASSESSING DEPRESSION IN ANGER-PRONE CHILDREN

What can mental health experts and educators do to make certain they don't "miss" depression as a causative factor in oppositional, anger-driven behavior? The first step has already been accomplished by you, the reader. It is important to *know* that there is a high rate of depression (between 21 and 83 percent) associated with anger-prone students.

Second, when working with aggressive and acting out youth, *assume* that there is depression until you can rule it out. Use Beck's cognitive triad of depressive thinking and simply ask the child or adolescent if he or she believes any of the statements to be true. (Examples: "Do you ever think you're worthless or unlovable?"; "Do you ever believe the world is a totally rotten place and it's never going to get any better?") Although it is true that some of these children can be very closed off and even dishonest about their feelings, there are many who are just waiting for the questions to be asked. They would be very willing to open up, but no one has bothered to try.

Finally, there are depression inventories that only take a few minutes to complete and can be used as a type of "depression screening." The Beck Depression Inventory (BDI) is used with respondents fourteen and older, and the Children's Depression Inventory (CDI) can be used for younger students. Even though these instruments are relatively short and only take a few minutes, they are fairly reliable indicators of depression.

When dealing with depression, it is important to help children and adolescents analyze the thoughts that sabotage their lives, because the beliefs they hold about themselves have as much, if not more, to do with their day-to-day functioning than any other variable. The real secret is not to get children and adolescents to merely *feel* better, because that will allow only limited relief. After the depression is recognized, the challenge lies in helping kids *think* better.

CONCLUSION

Depression is often present, but misdiagnosed, in angry and aggressive students. A meta-analysis by Angold and Costello (1983) reported that between 21 and 83 percent of children diagnosed as either ODD or CD also exhibited symptoms of depression. Beck and Shaw (1977) referred to the beliefs leading to depression as the "cognitive triad." These beliefs are 1) negative view of self, 2) negative view of the world, and 3) negative view of the future. Practitioners are encouraged to carefully consider the possibility that angry and acting out students may be suffering from depression.

CHAPTER 9

Transcriptions

This chapter contains transcriptions of three sessions with a fourth-grade male. John was referred to an anger control group I was conducting, but due to the limited number of spaces, he was not included in the group at the times these sessions were recorded.

John had been a concern to his fourth-grade teacher due to his problem with anger, but also because of his tendency to create rather elaborate lies. The fabrications were what I like to call "crazy lies." Some lies have an obvious intention, such as avoiding punishment, which is a concern but at least makes some sort of sense. The goal is to avoid punishment. Crazy lying is the type of lying that does not appear to have a purpose other than to impress others.

This child had the type of anger problem that was not a daily concern. He would hold his anger in until he exploded in a fit of rage. Usually when this occurred he was under some type of stress at home. John was a likable boy and seemed to pick up on the REBT concepts quickly.

SESSION 1

Therapist: When we were walking down here you said you got in trouble and then I asked you a little bit about what happened there. So go ahead and start back with what you were saying.

John: O.K. See I went to the bathroom but they were being too loud but Chris pushed me into the door, I mean into that thing that you . . .

T: Paper towel?

J: Yeah, and I hit my head and I almost got in trouble for that but see, you're not allowed to go in the bathroom . . . or, if it's too loud you have to get out.

T: O.K.

J: And see I went in it and I was trying to get out and Chris just goes, "Your mother is fat" and all that and Mrs. Townsend heard and . . . .

T: So you almost got in trouble for that.

J: And I go, I had to talk to Mrs. Swenson (the principal) and Mrs. Smith (his teacher) said, "Why don't you just let them go because I think they learned a lesson." That was me and Billy, Chris, and Tim and . . . .

T: So you didn't get in trouble but you almost did. You were saying that, what teacher did you almost get in trouble with? Mr. Black?

(Author's Note: It became clear that this story was not leading anywhere, so I interrupted and tried to move the discussion to another topic. One of the advantages of REBT is that it is very problem focused and does not promote the notion that the therapist must listen to endless stories from the client. Practitioners are free to be very active with the client and direct the session where they feel it needs to go.)

J: No, Smith.

T: Oh, but there was a different time. Not in the bathroom.

J: Um . . . what time was it?

T: That you might have to serve a detention.

J: That was Mrs. Swenson.

T: Mrs. Swenson . . . . O.K.

J: And she said to me and Tim because Chris had said, "Stay away from me" and he hit Billy with a baseball bat and Billy hit him back.

T: So you guys all got sent to the office.

J: Yeah, we all had to go talk to Mrs. Swenson. And she said me and Billy could go back to class cause she thought we learned our lesson and we did.

T: Good.

J: Tim got an after school detention.

(Author's note—I never did quite understand what went on with the baseball bat, paper towel holder, etc., but John was not bothered by what had transpired so I moved ahead once again.)

T: What I wanted to talk to you a little bit about today is how sometimes we get angry about stuff and that can lead to other kinds of problems. Now let me ask you, see if you can think back to a time when you got really angry about something. Something that happened in the last few days maybe or the last week or last month.

J: Last month when I got in trouble for my brother.

T: O.K. Tell me about that.

J: See he was ripping up my baseball cards and the cards were really good to me (Author's note—I took that last comment to mean the cards were really important to him.) and my mom said, "Stop him from doing that" and I got really angry and started calling him names.

T: Uh-hum, this is your little brother, right?

J: Yeah.

T: So you got really angry. Were you more angry at your mom or at your little brother?

J: I was more angry at my little brother.

T: Yeah, because he was ripping stuff up. Were you also angry because you got in trouble and it wasn't really your fault?

J: Yeah.

T: Let me ask you about times here at school. Have you ever gotten into trouble here because you were really angry and you said something or did something that you probably shouldn't have done?

J: People were playing soccer, you know, out by the tennis courts and they were using hands.

T: They were cheating?

J: And you're not supposed to use hands and I said something inappropriate (Author's note—I was very surprised to have a fourth-grader use the phrase, "I said something inappropriate," but that was his choice of words.) like, "Knock it off, shut up" and all that and I got told on.

T: So you didn't get in real trouble but you were angry that they weren't playing the game the right way. That's not really fair that they were using their hands and stuff. What I want to try and help explain is that people think, I bet you think, that people using their hands and cheating at this game is what made you angry.

(Author's note—At this point it is time to introduce the concept of the ABCs.)

J: Yeah.

T: But you know what?

J: What?

T: Actually that's not quite right. It's something a little different. But that's what most people think, isn't it? Let me draw something here. We're going to say here at point "A" what happened was people were using their hands in soccer. How about we just put down people were cheating at soccer. Down here at point "C" you were really angry. O.K.?

Now like I said, what most people think is that at point "A," people cheating at soccer, causes you to be angry at point "C." Actually there is a middle part, here at "B," that happens that actually makes you angry. But let me tell you a story to see if I can help explain this. Let's pretend you and I are going to go on a trip on a bus. Where are we going to go?

J: The Ozarks.

T: The Ozarks, all right, the Ozarks on a bus. So were riding on a bus and you're sitting in the middle and I'm by the aisle and there is somebody by the window. All of a sudden, for no reason, you get poked in the ribs. It's a real hard poke that really hurts.

J: Did he mean to poke me?

T: Let's not worry about that just now. How would you probably feel if you got poked in the ribs?

J: Mad.

T: O.K. Good and mad and probably angry so we put that down here at "C" and it's the same idea that we just talked about that people think getting poked in the ribs is what makes you angry. But now you're angry and your ribs hurt and you turn around and you look and you see that it was a blind man and he was taking off his sweater because he was hot and he accidentally poked you right in the ribs cause he couldn't see you. What do you think you'd feel at that point?

J: Sad.

T: Maybe even sad. Why do you think you'd feel sad?

J: Because he's a blind person and he didn't mean to do it and probably felt bad for it.

T: Now you know what is really interesting is that getting poked in the ribs, that still happened, didn't it? But you feel two different ways, don't you? At first when you thought he did it on purpose you were mad, weren't you? But then when you saw it was a blind man you were sad because he didn't mean to and he's blind. Now you know what that shows us? There must be a middle part, "B" that changes to change how you feel? Do you understand me?

J: Yeah.

T: Explain it to me.

(Author's note—As I've pointed out elsewhere in this book, a client can say he or she understands but not be clear regarding a concept. It is always a good idea to check for understanding, especially when you are introducing important concepts.)

J: There must be a middle part to make you feel two different things.

T: Right. Let's look at that a little closer. When you first got poked and were mad and angry. What could you have been thinking to yourself to make yourself angry about being poked in the ribs?

J: It was on purpose.

T: So it was on purpose. (Author's note—I wrote down the first part even though I knew there was a second irrational belief that follows this initial statement. The belief, "It was on purpose" is probably irrational as well because there is no proof that the poke was intentional.) What are you saying to yourself about people poking people in the ribs on purpose? "He poked me in the ribs on purpose and . . . ." (Author's note—This is an example of the "complete the sentence" technique that can help clients find that second, irrational belief that can exist without the client's awareness.)

J: I felt bad.

T: O.K., let me see if I can help. See if you can use this word to finish the sentence. Try to use the word "should" or "shouldn't" when you finish the sentence. He poked me in the ribs on purpose and . . . .

J: He shouldn't have done it.

(Author's note—John was like a lot of clients. On their initial exposure to REBT they need assistance finding the irrational belief. The goal is to help the client get to the point where he or she can do this easily without any outside assistance.)

T: He shouldn't have done it. That's exactly right. Let me put that down. You know what? You know why I know that word "shouldn't" is real important? Because whenever we're getting really mad and angry, do you know what is going on?

J: You shouldn't do it.

T: (Laughing.) What's really going on is that we're demanding that somebody act differently than they acted. Aren't we? When we say, "He shouldn't have done it," aren't we kind of saying, "I demand that he not do this?"

J: Yeah.

T: And you know the problem with that?

J: You're demanding something from other people and they might not agree with you.

(Author's note—It is rare for a ten-year-old to be able to spontaneously make a rational statement like the one John had just made. If your clients don't catch on as quickly, don't be alarmed. John was a good client to work with and that's why I chose his session to use in this chapter.)

T: That's exactly right. Who controls how this guy on the bus acts? Do we?

J: No.

T: Who does?

J: Him.

T: He does, doesn't he? And whenever we demand that other people act a certain way, it's sort of like we're pretending to be God, isn't it? Sort of like we're going, "I am God and I demand that you not do this." And like you said, we're not God and we don't control them. Now, here's the second part of this. You looked over and saw that he was a blind person, right? And you instantly thought something else. What did you probably think to make yourself feel sad or at least not be mad?

J: He was taking off his sweater and he didn't mean to hit me.

T: Didn't mean to hit me.

J: It was an accident.

T: That's right. It was an accident. And you see how once you thought, "It was an accident," your anger went away right away, didn't it? Right away you said you felt sad instead of mad. Now let's take what we're talking about with the blind man and move it up here to people cheating on soccer. Remember we're talking about people using their hands, which is against the rules and you got angry and mad. What do you think you were saying to yourself about people cheating that made you angry? See if you can use that word again.

J: That they shouldn't do it because that's cheating.

T: That's right. They shouldn't do it because that's cheating. That's really good. Now you know what, how could we change this demand, this "shouldn't," to more of a wish or preference? Do you know what the word preference means? It's a big word and it sort of means if you had your choice between steak and pizza, which would you prefer?

J: Pizza.

T: O.K., you'd choose pizza. So instead of saying, "I demand steak or I demand pizza," if you said, "I would prefer to have pizza." How could we change that "should" or "shouldn't," what kind of word could we use?

J: I'd prefer that they wouldn't use hands in soccer.

T: (Writing this down.) I'd prefer that they wouldn't use hands in soccer. Now, can you see that the real difference between these two is that

"They shouldn't do it because that's cheating" . . . that's a commandment, isn't it? We talked about pretending we're God. But if you said, "I'd prefer that they wouldn't use hands in soccer," or do you know another word you could use? I wish they wouldn't.

J: That's what I was going to say.

T: You were going to say that? O.K. I wish they wouldn't but they can. Do you see how that would make you a lot less angry?

J: Yeah.

T: That's really good. You picked up on that really well. But I knew you would because you're a bright young man. Now which do you prefer, soccer or baseball?

J: I prefer both.

T: Good. You know what? Whenever you find yourself getting really angry about something, if you can stop and listen to what you are saying to yourself, I'll almost guarantee there will be a "should" or a "must" or a "ought to" or a "have to" or any of those. If you can stop and listen to those, you know what? You won't be as angry. If you can change those "shouldn'ts" into words like "I wish" or "I prefer" or another phrase might be, "It would be better if people didn't cheat in soccer but people are going to do what they are going to do." It's sort of like it would have been better if Chris wouldn't have pushed you into the towel holder but you or I or even Mrs. Swenson can't control what Chris does. Do you understand that?

J: Yep.

T: What I think we ought to do is get together next week and talk some more. Would you like that?

J: Yeah.

T: I want you to look for a situation where you might make yourself angry and try really hard to listen for those "shoulds" and "shouldn'ts" and see if you can't change them into "wishes." Can you try [to] do that?

J: Yes.

Summary of Session 1

John was a motivated client and picked up on the logic of REBT quickly. As I said, sessions don't always go this well, and this one was especially enjoyable because it was the first time he had been introduced to these ideas. I have found that a solid approach using the following sequence of activities is useful for the first session:

1. Ask clients for an anger problem or a situation in which they anger themselves (i.e., identify and get the client to agree upon the "A").
2. Get the client to describe the emotion, or "C."
3. Explain that "A" does not cause "C"; there is a middle part, "B."
4. Use the "blind man on the bus" story to illustrate that "B" causes "C."
5. Move the logic of "the blind man" to the problem the client presented.
6. Help the client identify the "B" that is causing anger.
7. Help the child change the IB into a RB.
8. Give the client a homework assignment to practice using the new RB.

SESSION 2

T: Do you remember what your homework assignment was for this week?

J: No.

T: It was to try to see, we were talking about anger . . . .

J: Oh, yeah, that's right.

T: Now do you remember?

J: Yeah.

T: See if you can tell me what your homework assignment was.

J: You told me to see if I could do what we talked about.

T: Right, I wanted you to try to think of a situation where you might normally have gotten angry and to keep yourself from getting angry.

J: Like I did on the soccer field.

T: Well, let me hear about it. Tell me exactly what you did.

J: Well, I didn't say . . . .

T: First tell me what happened and then tell me what you did to keep from getting angry.

J: People were saying swear words when someone would score a goal or something and I said, "I wish you wouldn't say swears" and they just said, "O.K." Then we played and I said, "I'll tell the teacher if you say swears" but I didn't get mad.

T: Right.

J: They just said things like, "Oh, shoot."

T: So not real swears?

J: Yeah.

T: But kind of like swears. So what did you do about that? What did you think?

J: I thought it was nice that they stopped it.

T: If they had continued to use swear words, what could you have thought to yourself to not make yourself angry?

J: I can always go tell the teacher.

T: O.K., you could have told the teacher, but what could you have thought to yourself instead of thinking, "they have to not swear" or "they shouldn't swear." What could you have thought to yourself?

J: They shouldn't swear.

T: O.K., but if you use "shouldn't" that's still a demand and you'd probably still get angry.

J: I wish.

T: I wish they wouldn't use swear words.

J: But it's their body and it's a free country.

T: That's right, and you know who controls their mouth and their voice? They do, don't they?

J: You can't go outside and talk it over and say, "I'm going to quit this right now." See my dad smokes and he tried to quit and you know those pads that you put on your arm?

T: Yeah.

J: He went in the sun one day and it burned him. So he took it off. My mom and I wish he would quit it because it can lead to damage, but now when he smokes he goes outside.

T: So at least he doesn't smoke in the house.

J: Well, sometimes he does. But he goes in a different area.

T: You know what really impresses me? You realize that if your dad is going to smoke, he's going to smoke. You can either really, really upset yourself about that, which isn't going to change whether or not he smokes . . . .

J: My mom used to smoke but my brother coughed when she smoked. Then he would turn his nose up so my mom quit and I was really happy but that doesn't make my dad quit.

T: That's right. And like I was just saying, whether or not you upset yourself, is that going to make your dad quit?

J: No.

T: No, probably not.

J: My dad has tried to quit twice.

T: He's tried to so maybe he will.

J: Have you ever seen an ashtray that can pull in the smoke?

T: Yes, I know what you mean.

J: We're trying to find one for him so he can smoke and be in the living room.

T: And it won't go all over the house. That's a good idea. I used to see those on television. Maybe you'll see a commercial with it on.

J: My mom is trying to find one.

T: It's really good that you're thinking real clearly about this. If people want to swear on the soccer field, they're going to do that. You wish they wouldn't but they have the right to. It's a free country like you said. And also what you're thinking about your dad smoking. "I wish he wouldn't. I hope he quits but I'm not going to ruin my life worrying about this and demanding he quit." Who's the only person you can really demand anything from and expect to get something?

J: Me.

T: That's right.

J: I know I'm not going to smoke but I want to get an earring, though.

T: You want to get an earring. Do you think my earring looks good?

J: Yeah.

T: O.K.

J: I really want to get an earring but my dad won't let me.

T: Maybe when you're a little older.

J: He said if I get an earring I have to wear a dress to school.

T: (Laughing.) I was a lot older than you when I got an earring. I was in college.

J: My mom thinks I should be old enough to pay for my own earring. But I'm not using my college money.

T: That's probably not a good idea. My dad wasn't real happy when I got my earring either. But he got over it eventually.

J: I have enough money to go to college and I don't want to spend it because I want to go to college so bad.

T: Well if you really want to then you probably will.

J: You know Larry Johnson? He could have played earlier but he stayed in college. I got the card of him when he was in college and I was really happy. I want to be like that.

T: You want to go to college.

J: Yeah, I want to be in the NBA just like Larry Johnson.

T: That sounds like a good goal to have. You know what is a good idea? To get a college degree just in case you don't make the pros. You can get a good job anyway.

J: Yeah, you can be a lawyer and get a Lamborghini. Did you know doctors can get any kind of car they want? The kind of car I want is a Lamborghini.

T: You have to make a lot of money to have one of those. You know what I'd like to know? How are you going to remember some of the lessons we learned? What are you going to do to think about those things over the summer?

J: I'll probably . . . . I'm not sure.

T: Can you remind yourself when you get angry?

J: Yeah.

T: What will you think to yourself?

J: I'll think that every time they do something I don't like I'll try to think "I wish" instead of "he should."

T: Try to keep those "shoulds" from becoming too common and keep them to wishes and preferences.

J: Yeah.

T: That will keep you a lot calmer. You won't have the same kind of problems with getting mad. That's a good goal to have. I'll probably see you one more time before the summer vacation but if I don't, have a great summer. I'll see you for sure next fall because you'll be back and I'll be back. Let's get you back to class now because I don't want you to miss too much English.

Summary of Session 2

John had an opportunity to practice his rational belief on the soccer field and seemed to do a pretty good job of becoming only irritated when another player used swear words. He wanted to spend time talking about things such as his father's smoking and college plans, which are not directly related to the presenting problem. What I've found over the years is that students desire a few minutes of your time to talk about things other than the presenting problem. Although REBT is very problem focused, it does not mean that a few minutes of a session cannot be used to hear about the client's life in other areas that are unrelated to his or her difficulty. Remember, a majority of the clients are not self-referred. John did not seek me out for help, I went to him.

There are usually opportunities to reinforce REBT concepts even in an apparently unrelated story. Note that I tried to help John see that it wouldn't do any good to get angry about his father's smoking because his father was the person who was responsible for his smoking. His father was either going to stop smoking or he wasn't. Getting upset about his smoking would have no impact.

SESSION 3

Therapist: So what have you been up to since we talked last?

J: Not really nothing. I slept over at a friend's house Friday and Saturday.

T: Whose house?

J: Billy's.

T: Was that fun?

J: Yeah, he has a Nintendo.

T: I bet you played that all night.

J: Not really. We played basketball outside.

T: Now do you play soccer in the summer?

J: Yes. Do you know if they are going to have the summer rec program this summer?

T: I've heard that, but I'm not sure if that's true or not. I know there's going to be swimming. I know that for sure.

J: My mom said there was going to be basketball, baseball, and swimming. And maybe soccer and football.

T: Well, I hope they do offer all that.

J: But it's going to cost more money.

T: Yeah. That's what I've heard, too.

J: So my mom said I can only do three sports.

T: So you're only going to play your top three.

J: You know Arnold. He was the life guard at Booth Lake last summer and he didn't think I could swim very good so he made me take a test. I passed it and now I can swim there whenever I want.

T: So now you can swim with everybody else?

J: Yeah, I can swim way out.

T: Good.

J: They thought I was too little.

T: Then you had to pass the test where you swim around the buoys for them.

J: Yeah.

T: Good.

J: Except I sort of cheated because the sand was so close to me when I was swimming that I kept on touching it so I kept on going.

(Author's note—I tried to spend a short amount of time at the beginning of this session catching up on John's activities since our last visit.)

T: You know what? What I wanted to talk about was what we talked about last time. About ways that we make ourselves angry. Can you tell me a little bit about what you remember what we talked about?

J: People cheating.

T: Right. People cheating at soccer, and things like that. You were saying that when people use their hands and cheat and things like that, you'd get angry. What I'm wondering is, can you remember what you say to yourself to make yourself angry?

J: What was the question again?

T: Do you remember what you say to yourself to make yourself really angry? Do you remember the key words "should" or "shouldn't?"

J: They shouldn't do it because that's cheating.

T: Yeah. Remember how we talked about that's kind of a demand that people should do this or they shouldn't do that.

J: It's like pretending you're God and you're saying, "The world has to be destroyed."

T: Right. Except instead of saying, "The world has to be destroyed," you're saying "People shouldn't cheat at soccer."

J: A lot of people do it though. It's kind of a free country, too.

T: What do you mean by that?

(Author's note—I knew what John meant but it's helpful to get the client to verbalize his or her rational ideas.)

J: People are free and they can do whatever they want.

T: It would be nice if people would do the right thing, wouldn't it?

J: A lot do the right thing.

T: That's right. But they don't have to, do they?

J: Because they're the best and they think they can do anything. Like Mike, he got adopted when he was five and now he has a mom and dad. Then he used his hands on the last goal and everybody was happy, but that was still cheating.

T: So they were happy even though he cheated to win. And you were kind of mad about that.

J: They say he can do anything.

T: Well, it is true that people can do what they want, pretty much. But it would be nice if people didn't cheat. Kind of like we said last time, "I wish they wouldn't use hands but if they really want to they can anyway." Like you said, it's a free country and people can do what they want. Can you think of a time since the last time we talked where you've gotten angry about something other than soccer?

J: Like people swearing? People use the "S" word, the "F" word.

T: Right on the field, huh?

J: I know one kid who swears a lot.

T: So you end up feeling how about people swearing? Do you end up feeling angry?

J: Kind of.

T: Kind of angry.

J: I'm kind of used to it.

T: Let me ask you this. Listen real close because this is important. If you had to rate how angry you might feel if people swore, if you rated it between 0, which means not angry at all, and 100, how angry would you be?

J: About 50.

T: About 50. Let me ask you another question. How angry do you think it is O.K. to feel if people swore? What number would you give that? Do you understand what I mean?

J: Yeah. I'd rate it a little bit higher.

T: So you don't even get as angry as you think it's O.K. to get when people swear. Is that kind of what you are saying?

J: Yeah.

T: O.K.

(Author's note—The goal of this procedure is to determine if the client is angry or irritated. I asked John first to rate how angry he was (50). He then reported that he felt it would be appropriate to be even a little angrier than 50. Since his rating was below what he considered an appropriate level of anger, it is a pretty good indication that his response is appropriate for the situation.

If clients reported that they would rate their anger at 85 and they felt an appropriate level would be 100 when people committed some misdeed, it still may be an inappropriate response. By stating that they consider 100 to be an appropriate response to some misdeed, the clients are still demanding that people not commit misdeeds.)

J: My mom would probably be at 100.

T: Your mom would be all the way to 100. She doesn't allow any swearing at all. That's probably a good idea. So what you're saying is that even though you get a little bit angry, it's a level of anger that you feel is about right for what happened. And it's O.K. to get a little bit angry. We call that irritated. Do you know what irritated means?

J: It means that you're sort of angry but not really angry.

T: Yeah. You're a little upset that people are acting in a way you don't like but you're not really, really angry like you're ready to hit something.

J: It's like I'm bothered by it.

T: That's a good word. Bothered.

J: Because I don't like to hear other people talk that way, swearing and all that, like they think everybody talks like that.

T: You think they want you to swear.

J: They want everybody to act the same way as they act.

T: What would it mean if they decided that because you don't do what they want you to do, like you don't swear, do you think they would really stop liking you?

J: No.

T: Probably not. If they were really friends they wouldn't stop liking you. Let me ask you this, now just pretend for a second, what if they stopped liking you? What would that prove about you?

J: I'd kind be sad.

T: O.K., you'd be sad because you might not have as many friends to play with. But let me ask you this, would it mean that you're a rotten person?

J: No.

T: How come?

J: Because I don't want to say swears just because other kids do.

T: And that would just mean that you don't always go along with what everybody else does. That's O.K.

J: My mom won't let me swear.

T: Sometimes other people just aren't going to like us. Wouldn't it be kind of boring if everybody liked us? Let me ask you this, can we do anything to make people like us?

J: Not really.

T: Probably not. And the really important part is that what other people think of us isn't as important as we sometimes make it out to be. Do you know what I mean? Can you explain what I mean by that?

J: Can you say that again?

T: Sure. What other people think of us isn't really as important as we make it out to be sometimes. Because we think, "If so and so doesn't like me it means I'm a real nerd or a dork." And it really doesn't mean that, does it? See if you can explain that to me?

J: Just because somebody calls you a name you don't have to get mad about it.

T: You know what I say about that? If somebody called you a watermelon, it wouldn't make you a watermelon, would it? That's kind of silly isn't it? If somebody calls you a dork, big deal.

J: It's a free country.

T: That's right. You don't have to get mad at all.

Summary of Session 3

John appeared to be making good progress with his anger. Obviously, many more sessions will be needed to help him generalize this basic understanding of REBT to real world success in anger management. It's clear that by the end of session 3, John had a good basis from which to work.

The latter half of the session was spent assessing his self-acceptance. Many students feel that if others don't accept them, they can't accept themselves. John does not appear to suffer from this need for approval, which is a positive indicator for his overall emotional development.

CHAPTER 10

Anger Control Groups
and Classroom Lessons

Chapter 9 provides a detailed overview of the early stages of individual therapy with a student having anger problems. An in-depth analysis often helps readers learn how the interventions are actually applied during a session. It's one thing to read about techniques but another to eavesdrop on a session to observe how a therapist operates during counseling.

The length of treatment often depends on the motivation of the student and the severity of the problem. John did not appear to have the type of anger problem that was seriously interfering with his daily life. However, he did have several difficulties both in and out of school that appear to have been anger related. Fortunately, he had not progressed from anger to violence, but if his difficulties had gone untreated, who knows? The type of demanding attitude he possessed could have allowed him to make that transition.

ANGER CONTROL GROUPS

Anger is a significant problem in many students' lives. Therefore anger is also a problem for the teachers who deal with these students. Unfortunately, in these days of tight budgets, mental health resources are limited in education. Therefore, schools often choose to serve anger-prone students in groups rather than individually. Even working in groups rather than individually, there are usually more students who could benefit from such programming than there are groups available to serve them.

When the faculty in one of the elementary schools in my district was informed that there were going to be groups to help students control their anger, I was overwhelmed with referrals from teachers. It seemed that every teacher with a class of twenty-five had a handful of students with significant anger problems. The verbal and physical confrontations teachers had witnessed earlier in the year led these educators to believe that certain students would have fewer difficulties if they could learn to control their tempers.

If you work in a school and decide to run anger control groups, it might be a good idea to sit down with a principal or building administrator and choose the students you feel are most likely to benefit from the group. This can prevent the problem of teachers being upset when they have referred a half dozen students and none were selected to participate in the first group.

Not all students with anger problems are appropriate for group therapy. Some clients with severe problems can be included in group but should also be seen individually. After a few weeks in group you will have a good sense of who is understanding the REBT logic and who may need individual support.

Size of Group

The size of an anger control (AC) group is very important. Students in AC groups often have a difficult time controlling their behavior. It might be possible to run other groups with ten to twelve students, but those large numbers would mean disaster in an AC group.

These students usually not only have anger problems but are also very "needy" in other areas. They often seek attention inappropriately because many come from dysfunctional homes where they have learned that the easiest way to get attention is to act up.

Student groups have been a part of my practice from the beginning, and I have had the opportunity to facilitate groups on a wide variety of issues. Groups that focus on alcohol and drug dependency in the home, divorce groups, grief and loss groups, and substance abuse treatment groups all have their delicate areas. With anger control groups, one of the most difficult aspects is managing the behavior of the participants.

Over the years I have developed a few techniques to help control some of the more unruly group members.

The single most important thing the group leader can do to help control the behavior of the group is to keep the size of the group down. A reasonable number of clients for an AC group is between six and eight. When you exceed these numbers you can reach a point of diminishing returns. By wanting to include those two extra students, you compromise the utility of the group for all.

The Speaking Ball

A ball is passed around the group. The only individual with permission to speak is the person who is holding the ball. The exception is the group leader(s), who has the right to speak with or without the ball.

This technique may appear to be appropriate only with younger children, but it has been used on occasion with middle school students. One group in particular used the speaking ball for a few weeks, and their behavior was noticeably improved. Students were speaking one at a time and listening to each other. I told the group I didn't think they needed to rely on the ball anymore since they were acting more appropriately and being better listeners. As soon as the ball was eliminated, their behavior regressed back to its previous level. The next week the speaking ball was reintroduced and the group went smoothly.

Divide and Conquer

If you are co-facilitating a group, there are times when it is appropriate to divide the group into two smaller groups. Some activities work better this way because students have more of an opportunity to speak. The smaller numbers allow the facilitators to keep better control over students.

Time Out

When a member or members are acting inappropriately, it might be best to ask those individuals to leave the group for a short time out. This usually happens only once, then the rest of the group settles down.

Always reserve the right to send students back to class or to the office if they continue to act up.

Specialized Seating

After the first week of group you will have a good idea if there are going to be behavior problems in group and which participants are going to need help controlling their behavior. You may want to separate two students who have a difficult time sitting together.

One of the best techniques is to simply have the difficult student(s) sit at your side. Keeping students in immediate proximity to you usually keeps them in line. If they do act up you can redirect them in a manner that doesn't call attention to the situation and allows the group to continue without disruption.

Duration of Group Therapy

The duration of group therapy also must be taken into consideration. Rational-Emotive Behavior Therapy is very much a "teaching" therapy, and groups sometimes feel like small classrooms. Groups that operate in schools are not necessarily designed to be unending support groups. With AC groups, there are certain concepts to be taught and time allotted for students to practice these new skills. Eight to twelve weeks is usually sufficient time to cover the content necessary in AC groups. It might be advisable to schedule follow-up meetings every two weeks or once a month to check on the progress of the group members.

Co-Facilitation

Another consideration is whether to run the groups alone or to co-facilitate. This decision may be made for you when potential co-facilitators see the list of students who will be in the group! Potential group leaders may think the group will be unmanageable and you may be facilitating by yourself even if you would like some help.

There are several advantages to having a co-facilitator. With two adults in the room there may be fewer problems controlling the students' behavior. There is also another adult to help with the organization of the group (i.e., writing passes, making photocopies, etc.). As mentioned previously, many of these children come from dysfunctional homes and have never had the opportunity to observe two adults working together in a productive manner.

Co-facilitation also provides the opportunity to expose another counselor or teacher to REBT. My agenda as a professional psychologist is to teach as many people as possible about REBT. It is a very effective system in helping kids learn how to eliminate destructive behaviors and self-defeating emotions. I take advantage of every opportunity I get to work with a new professional if for no other reason than to spread the word about REBT.

There are also some potential problems with co-facilitation. If a co-facilitator does not agree with your approach, it would probably be unwise to run a group together. Conflicting ideas in the course of a group can lead to numerous other difficulties.

The Use of Confederates

It may be advisable to use what I call confederates in an AC group. Confederates are students who do not have significant anger problems but whose presence would be beneficial to the group. These individuals are usually students in the school who can be helpful by modeling appropriate problem-solving techniques. It is not necessary to tell the AC students why these students are in the group. They will assume they are in the group to learn to control their anger, like everyone else. Anger is such a common emotion that the confederates usually have no difficulties sharing personal examples of when they became angry like the other group members.

Meet with confederates for a few weeks before the group starts to teach them about REBT. An excellent resource is *A Rational Counseling Primer,* by Howard Young (1974), which can be given to the confederates and may also be used in the group. The confederates need to have a good understanding of the ABCs as well as the most commonly occurring irrational ideas leading to anger.

The potential benefits of using confederates in group include the following:

1. They can model appropriate behavior in group.
2. They can be used to help clarify important points.
3. They can demonstrate appropriate problem-solving approaches.

If there have been AC groups operating previously in your school, there may be a student who has been in an earlier group who will sign up for group again. This is not only helpful by providing a confederate, it means the credibility of the group is strong. These students have a tendency to believe the group is beneficial, and they often bring with them their friends who need help.

Referrals

At the middle and high school level, the best way to make certain that all students have the opportunity to refer themselves to an AC group is to make brief presentations to all students in their classrooms. This seems like a monumental task, but it's not if you have several professionals making these five- to ten-minute presentations. Every student in our high school had to be in some type of English class, so by doing these short presentations in all the English classes we knew we had reached every student in the building.

Many schools encourage students to stop in the guidance office if they would like to get information about educational support groups. The problem with this approach is that there are many students who will not have the courage to stop in to make an appointment to talk with a counselor. They may be worried that their friends will tease them about talking to counselors. By forcing them to take the initiative rather than going to their classrooms directly, your program may miss students who would benefit from the group.

The presentation can include the reasons the school is offering a group for students who have problems with anger. I usually give a few examples of the negative effects of anger on health and relationships. Explain that the information students divulge in group is confidential and their attendance at group is voluntary. Details can also be provided regarding the location and length of the group.

It is highly recommended that a sign-up sheet be distributed to each student at the beginning of the presentation. Students can then be instructed to put their names on the paper and mark the appropriate box that they are either "interested in receiving more information " or "not interested at this time." All students hand in a slip at the end of the presentation, so others won't know who is going to attend the group.

The reason for using the slip of paper is to avoid the stigma of having to raise their hands. Confidentiality also extends to the students interested in the group. Attending group can be embarrassing for many students.

Individual Meetings Prior to Group (a.k.a. Screening)

Potential group members can be contacted before the group's initial session. The purpose of this screening is to answer questions and assess each student's motivation to be in the group.

As has been stated throughout this book, unless clients acknowledge that they have a problem with anger, it is difficult to help them. Acknowledgment is only the first step. Clients must also be willing to change how they look at the world, because the world certainly isn't going to change for them.

Remember that for every one slot available, there are probably ten students who could benefit from such a group. If a client doesn't appear genuinely motivated to be in the group, his or her slot could prove more beneficial to another student. Students may be interested in the group just to get out of class. Always reserve the right to ask any member to leave the group if his or her behavior or attitude is detrimental to the goals of the group. This rarely happens, because if a client isn't enjoying the group experience, he or she usually does not return.

Even if students are not taking responsibility for their anger, there are techniques that can raise a student's motivation to change. Some students view anger as a source of power. For short periods of time anger can allow individuals to get what they want by intimidating and bullying others. That is one reason why anger can be a difficult problem to overcome. Students are immediately reinforced for their anger and do not experience the negative consequences until much later.

Some students will view controlling their anger as a sign that they are a "wimp." Counselors need to make certain students understand that anger control is actually empowering. Students who let others control how they feel have less power than students who can manage their emotions.

There are very few people who know the things that the group members can learn through an AC program. The ideas to be learned are like well-kept secrets, and the participants can benefit from this information if they are willing to learn.

Most of the information children and adolescents learn in school is quickly forgotten and is perceived by students as having no relevance to their lives. The ideas students can learn in an AC group can be beneficial for the rest of their lives and may keep them out of serious trouble.

By middle school and high school, most of the potential AC group members will have had some type of contact with the school's disciplinarian (often the assistant principal) or the legal system. As adjudicated delinquents, these students have a court deposition that states what is expected of them while on probation. I have told several potential AC members that the group experience may be the only thing keeping them out of prison. The jails are filled with people who have anger problems, and the department of corrections will certainly make room for one more. When students see the group experience as being directly beneficial to them, they are more likely to make a commitment to work in group.

It's important to try to help these students see how their anger causes difficulties in their lives. Many of their problems in school, at home, and with their peers are at least partially related to their anger difficulties. In one way or another, they are eventually going to have to deal with the problem.

If they agree to enroll in group, I present a contract for them to look over and sign if they agree to the terms. A copy of this contract is in appendix A. They will be expected to live up to the terms of the contract. If they do not plan to follow the contract, they need not sign it.

Parental Permission

The need to acquire written parental permission to conduct educational support groups varies from state to state. Parents should be aware that such programs operate within the school, and if they would *not* like their child to participate in such groups, they should notify the school.

Our district explains in the student handbook the various student assistance programs (SAP) that are run in our schools. We also have monthly newsletters that often contain information regarding upcoming groups. This is an excellent way to allow parents to refer their children for AC groups or other SAP groups.

Many districts must seek written permission from parents to include children in groups. This can keep some students out of groups because their parents refuse to grant permission. These students are often troubled because they come from dysfunctional families. The parents of these families do not want anyone knowing what goes on in their homes.

The permission slip should be written in simple language. A sample of a parental permission form appears in appendix G.

Always include a self-addressed stamped envelope if you decide to mail these home rather than have the children carry them. Once you've received permission slips back you are ready to start the group.

GROUP LESSONS

Lesson 1

A great deal of business usually must be taken care of during the initial week of group before the lessons can begin. In smaller districts, all of the students usually know each other, but if some group members aren't acquainted, introductions are in order. Students can state their name, grade, what they would like to be called in group, and what they are hoping to get out of group (i.e., their goals). For my sake more than theirs, I do not proceed until every member can name every other member.

After introductions, it is best to hand out schedules of the following meetings. Any other group business, such as receiving a pass to come to group or the location of next week's group, can be covered at this time.

This is also the time to establish group rules, some of which were outlined in the group contract. It is always advisable to get the students to make up the rules. After all, this is their group, and they deserve to have a say in the procedures. It is best to place the group rules on a large sheet of paper or posterboard that will remain on a wall in your meeting room for the duration of group. Sample rules follow:

1. Be on time.
2. What is said in group, stays in group (confidentiality).
3. No personal attacks or "slams."
4. Only one person speaks at a time.
5. Everyone has the right to "pass" or not participate in an activity.

The importance of confidentiality can't be overemphasized. Take a few minutes to make certain the participants understand that being able to feel safe sharing personal information is extremely important. It is not a break in confidentiality for the students to share what *they* spoke about in group, but they should not share what other people said or mention the names of other group members. They can tell people in general terms what went on in group as long as they leave out specific details.

Rate Your Week

An "icebreaker" activity I use in every group I run is called "Rate Your Week." Students take turns giving their week a number between 1 and 10 and then explain why their week was a "4" or a "7." During the initial week of group try to plan activities that require participation to let everyone hear their voices in the room. Some students may be anxious about speaking in front of other students, but my guess is there won't be too many "shy" members in your AC group.

Before any lessons begin it is a good time to pretest the students with the Anger Survey (see appendix B). This is a short instrument that will allow you to chart the effectiveness of the group in reducing the anger of the participants.

Lesson for the Week: Thoughts Cause Feelings

Most people believe that events cause feelings. Although events have a definite impact on the emotions experienced, the thoughts, beliefs, and attitudes individuals carry play a dominant role in determining the feelings they will experience. The best way to illustrate this point is through using a group member's recent experience. Ask for someone to give you an example of when he or she made himself or herself angry. Record the "A" and the "C."

A—Got detention in science class.
C—Angry.

Explain that "A" did not cause "C." As much as it may seem that way, there is a middle part ("B") that actually caused "C." Ask if it would be possible for someone to get detention and not be angry. This is an excellent opportunity to use your confederates, if you have them. If the other group members are not able to give you an example of a student being happy about receiving detention, make one up. A student could be happy he received detention because a girl he likes also will be in that same detention period and he may get to talk to her. If the student has after school detention, he will not have to go home and work around the house, which might be worse than detention.

Usually students can come up with several emotions other than anger that they might experience after receiving detention. If students report different emotions (such as sadness or anxiety), explain that their feelings are different because they are thinking different thoughts to produce these emotions. Students could be sad that they received detention because they will miss an after-school event they had been looking forward to. Anxiety could result from students who know that they will be grounded if their parents find out.

Tell the "blind man on the bus" story (see chapter 9) and perform an ABC analysis:

A—Got poked in the ribs.
B—"People shouldn't poke other people in the ribs."
C—Angry.

Then explain that the man who did the poking was blind and didn't mean to hurt anyone. Because he was blind he couldn't see other passengers and therefore the action was unintentional. Perform an ABC analysis with this new information.

A—Got poked in the ribs.
B—"It was an accident. He didn't mean to poke me."
C—Not angry, pity, ashamed, etc.

Many students will report that when they were told the man was blind, not only were they no longer angry but they now felt 1) pity for the man and/or 2) ashamed that they were angry in the first place.

The stage has now been set for making the important point that events (getting poked in the ribs) can't completely cause emotions (anger, pity, shame). How could the same event at point "A" (getting poked in the ribs) cause several different emotions at point "C?" Just as was done with John in chapter 9, transfer this logic to the example given in group by the student.

A—Got detention in science class.
B—"I shouldn't have gotten detention. It's not fair and I have to be treated fairly."
C—Anger.

Using the same "A" (getting detention), try changing the "B" to a rational belief to demonstrate the impact beliefs have on feelings at "C."

A—Got detention in science class.
B—"I wish I wouldn't have gotten detention. I don't think I deserved it and I'd like to be treated fairly, but everyone gets treated unfairly some of the time. Just because I'd like to be treated fairly doesn't mean I have the power over other people to make that come true."
C—Irritation and acceptance of situation.

Point out to the group that even though the event stayed the same, the feelings at "C" were very different depending on the thoughts at "B."

You can also try another activity to reinforce the idea that beliefs cause feelings by asking members to think of a situation that would have everyone in the group feeling the same way. When a group member states an event such as winning the lottery, ask the rest of the members if they can think of something *bad* about winning the lottery. They usually will be able to come up with an idea or two that would make winning the lottery unfavorable (such as tax problems), which would illustrate the point that nothing is either good or bad; our thinking makes it so.

Out-of-Group Practice

One of the resource books I have used is *A Rational Counseling Primer,* by Howard Young (1974). It's short and filled with many illustrations for the visual learner. Students often report that the book helped them with the concepts. Another book designed to be used as a curriculum for AC groups is my *Hot Stuff to Help Kids Chill Out. Hot Stuff* basically follows the curriculum presented in the remainder of this chapter. I've also run groups using neither book, instead relying on the worksheets in appendixes for the practice exercises. Either (or both) would be a good supplement but should not be considered essential.

If you use Howard Young's book, the group's practice activity is to read a portion of the book and write a paragraph or two about what they've read. You will probably hear some grumbling about "homework," which is to be expected. Let the group know that if they plan on getting the most out of this experience they are going to have to practice between sessions. It is clearly stated in the contract they signed that there will be occasional out-of-group homework.

To encourage homework completion, you may want to set up an agreement whereby the group can have a pizza party if they earn a certain percentage of the possible points. They can earn up to two points per member, per week, one point for attending on time and one point for completing their homework assignment.

I have used an incentive program with some groups, and it has helped with attendance and the completion of out-of-group assignments, but it is also extra work for the group leader. In addition, any incentive program runs the risk of causing students to focus their efforts on the reward and away from the real intention of the group, which is learning anger management skills. This is a decision that each group leader will have to make, but my advice is not to use an incentive program unless you feel it is essential to the success of the group.

Lesson 2

Start with "Rate Your Week," if you are going to use that exercise. I like to use this activity because it allows the facilitators to "check in" with the clients and also provides topics for discussion in the group. Students may state that they had a "2" because they got in a fight with their parents. It might be a good idea to perform an ABC analysis of what the students were thinking to get angry.

At the start of Lesson 2 it is appropriate to review the rules of the group one last time. This only takes a few minutes and will not need to be done unless a group member is violating one of the rules.

Check on the homework from Lesson 1. Does everyone have a paragraph about the book? Has each student either read his or her paragraph or described what he or she thought was the most important or main idea in the book? If there are missing assignments, why? If you decide to use an incentive program, this may be a good opportunity to use the pizza party to put some pressure on members who did not complete their homework. Encourage the group members to remind each other of the homework assignment during the week.

Lesson for the Week: Rational versus Irrational Beliefs

It is now time to help students learn to distinguish rational from irrational beliefs. With younger students, it may be wise to substitute "true" and "false" for "rational" and "irrational."

Emphasize the need for proof to substantiate that a belief is rational. The following example illustrates a a good method of teaching how proof is gathered.

Suppose a miracle diet pill was invented that promised to cause people to lose ten pounds overnight. How would the public know whether that belief would be true or false?

Students usually explain that there could be an experiment in which the pill is given to people (or animals) before they go to sleep at night.

In the morning, they could be weighed, and if they lost the ten pounds, that would be proof that the pill works and the belief would be true. If they didn't lose the weight, the belief would most likely be false.

The same search for proof can help people determine if other beliefs are true or false. The worksheet "Where's the Proof?" (see appendix C) can be completed in group. Students may not have sufficient time to finish the worksheet in group; if so their homework assignment is to complete the worksheet and bring it to class for Lesson 3. If they do finish the worksheet in group, a substitute practice activity is to have them explain to an adult how to determine if a belief is true or false. They usually select either their parents or teachers. To get a point credit, they have to get the adult to sign a note verifying that they attempted this activity.

Another exercise that can be beneficial is giving the group an "A" and asking them for examples of "Bs" and "Cs" that might accompany the event. Following are a few examples of "As" that might be used:

- Got a "C" on a science test.
- Family is moving to Florida.
- You are getting a job this summer.

This exercise is also helpful because not everyone will have the same "C." Some students would be very happy to be moving to Florida because they would think something such as, "It will be warm all year round and we will be close to Disneyworld." Others would be unhappy because they would think, for example, "We'll be leaving behind our friends and family."

Lesson 3

After "Rate Your Week" and checking on homework, go over the "Where's the Proof?" worksheet (appendix C). Spend time disputing why some beliefs are true and some are false.

Help the students learn to watch for key words such as *must, should, always*, etc. Pay particular attention to number 6 on the worksheet

("Other people make me feel bad."). This is certain to bring about disagreement among group members.

Lesson for the Week: People Make Themselves Angry

Use the "Anger Incident Worksheet" (see appendix D). Each member is to complete this sheet in group independently. After the students
have completed the sheet (which usually takes about six to eight minutes), go over their answers together. The first four questions are quite
simple and ask about the events leading up to their anger, but often
students will need help with questions 5 and 6, which ask about their
self-talk. Students have very little, if any, experience analyzing their
thinking, so this part of the exercise is difficult for most students.

The important part of this lesson is getting students to start listening
to their self-talk, which is producing their anger. Such thoughts occur
almost automatically and students do not realize they are thinking or
talking to themselves. As an incentive to get them to start listening to
their self-talk, they can earn an extra-credit point by writing down five
things they said to themselves during the week. These thoughts can be
related to anything and do not need to focus on anger. Try giving them
examples with which they might be able to identify. When they see a
new sports car, do they think, "I wish I had a car like that?" When
they get a long homework assignment do they think, "I hate school"
or "Now I can't go to the movies."?

The required out-of-group assignment for next week is to complete
an "Anger Incident Worksheet" using a different situation. It can be a
situation or event that just occurred or something that happened a while
ago.

Lesson 4

Once again, start by completing "Rate Your Week" and review the
previous week's homework. There may be some interesting homework
assignments to discuss. The important part of the "Anger Incident
Worksheet" has to do with the identification of irrational beliefs and
their disputations. Students are going to have to eventually learn to
complete these two important steps independently. At this point in the

group you will have some students who can find their IBs easily and others who are still struggling.

This is a skill unlike anything students have ever learned before, and it will take time to master. Be supportive and patient. Reinforce attempts to find and dispute IBs even if the students were less than perfect in their performance.

Major Lesson: "Let's Get Rational" Board Game

During lesson 4 the "Let's Get Rational" (LGR) board game is used. This is a pleasant way to reinforce the basic concepts of REBT. By this point in group students are tired of worksheets and practice. Unless they have some fun in group, they may not be returning for lesson 5. With LGR they can have a change of pace but still practice their new thinking skills.

This counseling board game can be used with both groups and individuals. It is designed for clients age eleven through adulthood, although students younger than eleven who are abstract thinkers can benefit from playing the game.

The game is played like most standard board games. A die is rolled and a player moves the required number of spaces and performs whatever action is requested on the square on which he or she lands. Approximately half of the squares have directions designed to encourage self-disclosure:

- Tell the group about a conflict you had this week.
- Tell the person to your left one thing you've learned about him or her through this group.
- Tell the group what is most on your mind today.
- Tell the group what you would like to improve about yourself.

The four Affirmation squares have a special purpose. When a player lands on an Affirmation square, the other players in the group take turns making one positive, affirming statement about the player. Finally, the player who landed on the square makes a self-affirming statement.

Affirmation squares can have a dramatic effect on the group. The sharing of affirming statements can be an emotional experience and can draw the group closer together.

Two Role Play squares are included. These squares are designed to give players practice performing an action that is difficult for them. Some of the Role Play cards focus on the ABC system:

- Perform an A, B, C, and D analysis of a situation in which you find it easy to make yourself angry.
- Perform an A, B, C, and D analysis of a situation in which you find yourself putting yourself down because of your behavior.

Other Role Play cards require group members to "act out" a situation:

- Role play being assertive in a situation in which it would be best to stand up for yourself.
- Role play resolving a conflict with a friend or family member.

Ten squares are entitled "Rational Reminder Pick up Cards." When a player lands on one of these squares, he or she is to pick from the pile of Rational Reminder Cards and read aloud the card's saying. For example:

- Life does not have to be better or different because you want it to be that way. You can either accept life or make yourself miserable with your own irrational thinking.
- No one likes frustration, but we can darn well stand it.
- There are no bad people, just people who at times act badly.
- We do not run the universe; therefore, we cannot get what we want just by demanding it.

The advantages of using "Let's Get Rational" are that

1. the game is enjoyable to play and counseling sessions are attended more regularly.
2. The game format is nonthreatening and encourages even the most resistant clients to "open up."

3. The forced communication of the squares and cards makes it acceptable for players to share personal information.
4. The game provides a many "teachable moments."
5. The game is ambiguous enough that almost any problem can be addressed through the cards and game squares. Some professionals have spoken of the "horoscope effect," whereby it seems as though every card is designed specifically for that particular group of players.

A research project examined the effectiveness of the game using eighty high school students as subjects. Forty experimental group subjects played the game one hour per week for seven weeks while forty control group subjects attended their regularly scheduled classes. Dependent measures included the Children and Adolescent Scale for Irrationality (CASI), the Beck Depression Inventory (BDI), and the Adjective Generation Technique (AGT), which is a measure of self-acceptance. Results indicated that subjects who played the game endorsed significantly fewer irrational beliefs than subjects in the control group. Ninth-grade subjects also exhibited more rational thought as measured by the CASI. Tenth-grade experimental subjects were significantly less depressed than tenth-grade control group subjects, according to scores on the BDI (Wilde, 1994).

"Let's Get Rational" is carried in many counseling catalogs, or you can write to the following address for information on obtaining a copy: LGR Publishing, 3219 NW "C" St., Richmond, IN 47374; (800) 369–5611.

Lesson 5

Usually out-of-group practice is not assigned after playing "Let's Get Rational" because the students have just had a fun week and assigning homework can ruin the upbeat mood. Week 5 is started with "Rate Your Week" or an optional icebreaker activity.

Lesson for the Week: Body Cues and Situational Triggers

It is important that group members learn to identify bodily cues that they are becoming angry. Each member is given an opportunity to share his or her own personal cues because many will be different. Appendix H is a worksheet designed to help students identify body cues.

Some will report that they feel warm before they become angry. Some may have reactions such as teeth clenching or fists tightening. Students can benefit from knowing their cues so that when they feel these changes taking place they can immediately identify and challenge their irrational beliefs. The key here is that they can learn to stop themselves *before* they become angry.

It is also important to help students identify when they are most likely to "lose it." In what types of situations do they find themselves most likely to become angry? Following is a list of situational triggers that are commonly listed by students:

1. When I am tired.
2. When I am not feeling well physically.
3. When I am under stress.
4. When things haven't been going well at home (i.e., parents fighting; arguing with siblings).
5. When I have been having difficulties with a significant other (i.e., boyfriend or girlfriend).
6. When a discussion involves a topic I feel passionately about.

Students can be made aware of their own situational triggers and encouraged to be aware of their tendency to become easily angered when they are involved with one or more of these. If they feel tired and are having some difficulties with their parents, they need to be extra sensitive to their bodily cues. Knowing their own tendencies can give them some extra time, almost a forewarning that could prevent them from "blowing their cool."

Two techniques that are easy to learn are deep breathing and counting backwards. When students are aware that they are becoming angry they can immediately take steps to avoid a rage state by taking some deep breaths. Slow, deep breaths have a calming effect. That's why basketball players use this procedure before shooting a foul shot. It is also helpful to say or think a calming word when they exhale. Students can think "relax" or "calm down" when they breathe out.

Counting backwards from ten or twenty is an age-old but helpful technique for reducing anger. It might be a good idea to tell group members to close their eyes when they are counting as well. Although these techniques fall in the category of "distractions," they are still beneficial in that they may give students time to think before reacting in an impulsive manner.

At some point in group it is a good idea to have the members generate a list of calming thoughts or phrases they can use when they feel themselves becoming angry. Some of the more popular suggestions are the following:

- "Chill."
- "Mellow out."
- "Be cool."
- "It's not worth it."

Out-of-Group Practice

Ask students to record a situation in which they might have become angry but were able to remain relatively calm. The reason for this homework assignment is to try to get students to focus on situations in which they have been able to control their temper, which gives the facilitator the opportunity to reinforce their hard work. It is also a great motivator to the students when they start to realize that *this stuff really works! I can keep myself from becoming angry!*

Lesson 6

Do "Rate Your Week" and share the group members' success stories. It is important for those in the group who are not as successful as others to realize that these skills take time to master. These students have had the habit of making themselves angry for years. They are not going to completely unlearn these habits in six lessons.

Following Lesson 6 is a good time to post-test the students using the "Anger Survey" (appendix B) to determine if they have learned the major concepts taught in the group. Now that the major lessons in group have been taught, it is time to use the weekly "Rate Your Week" to check each group member's progress. Group now becomes much less structured and the emphasis is on helping members cope with problems. Support from other members can be especially beneficial at this point. This is also an appropriate time to schedule follow-up meetings to check progress.

A good closing activity is to have students take turns sharing what they have learned in group. Also, each student can put his or her name on a piece of paper and have the other group members write something positive about him or her on it. I have done this activity, but instead of passing the papers around I have had the students pin them to their backs so the comments can be written while the paper is hanging from their shirts. Then each member can read aloud what was written about them. This can be a tremendously powerful experience for group members. Once again, support and encouragement from peers can be very motivating to students.

Before ending Lesson 6 I make sure each member has his or her personal rational coping statement written down. Encourage the students to write down their coping statements on index cards and place them in lockers, on mirrors, or in other locations where they will be seen daily.

ALTERNATIVE ACTIVITIES

Following are activities that can be substituted or added to the curriculum. After the third lesson it is never a bad idea to use the "Anger Incident Worksheet" (appendix D) as a review. During some weeks a lesson may go faster than you anticipated and you may have five minutes left before the period ends. Rather than waste this time, it is easy to ask the group, "Who's got a situation they got angry about that we could use to complete an Anger Incident Worksheet?" Usually it is not a problem finding situations to analyze.

As the group members get become experienced, it is also appropriate to do the ABC without the worksheet as a guide. Students won't be walking the halls with "cheat" sheets, so when you think the time is right, try walking them through the ABC without the assistance of the worksheet.

Hang Man

Divide the group in half and have teams take turns deciding if a statement is rational (true) or irrational (false). If a team answers incorrectly, a body part is added to their drawing of a stick person being hung. The first group whose person has all the body parts (head, torso, arms, legs, hands, and feet) is the loser.

Some may be concerned about an activity called "hang man" due to the violence associated with the term. This same type of activity can be conducted using a spider. The losing group is the first to have a body and eight legs.

Self-Acceptance Unit

Many of the AC clients view themselves as somehow less than adequate and generally believe they are "no good." Some group members are in considerable trouble at school and possibly in the community at large. They have been condemned for their behavior by most adults and have come to doubt their inherent value as human beings. These students often believe that because they have a tendency to behave badly and make poor choices, they are rotten people. Viewing themselves as less than adequate only leads to more difficulties and makes overcoming their anger problems that much more difficult.

Ellis (1977a) has pointed out that certain individuals use anger to mask depression and feelings of worthlessness. This is a distinct possibility and especially true at younger grades. Children in early elementary school have a difficult time verbalizing their feelings and tend to act out their frustration. Be aware that once you get beyond the rage there may be a good deal of depression and feelings of worthlessness.

Lesson: The Human Junkyard

The idea behind this lesson is to teach students that all individuals have both positive and negative qualities. Everybody has some things they do very well and other things they struggle with. Students would be foolish to rate themselves as totally worthless because they have problems in a few areas of their lives. The problem areas do not take away the positive qualities they have.

Pick a student and ask him, "If you could have any car in the world, which car would you pick?" When the student answers give him an opportunity to tell a few things about the car and explain why it is such an exceptional automobile. Next ask, "If you had this car and it had flat tires, would you throw the whole car into the junkyard?" When the student says, "No," explain that students are "junking" themselves when they think of themselves as worthless because they have a few problems. Having difficulties or family problems doesn't mean they are worthless, it just means they have got an area or two that needs repair, like a car with flat tires.

The car analogy is often most effective with boys because many boys love cars. Most of my clients in early AC groups were male (a.k.a., "the Mellow Fellows"). The same point can be made with females using the idea of a "perfect outfit." Would they throw away all the clothes if there were a single missing button?

Pie Graph Activity

Another activity designed to get students to stop berating themselves involves the use of a circular or pie graph. Draw a circle and ask a student to tell you what percentage of his or her behavior is "bad." Designate that area of the circle as bad behavior. Next ask what percentage of his or her behavior is "good." If he or she fails to give you two figures that add up to 100 percent, explain that the rest of the behavior is neutral, neither good or bad. Explain that for someone to be a "bad person" 100 percent of his or her behavior would have to bad. That is impossible because no one can act inappropriately all the time. If a student insists that he or she is bad 100 percent of the time, explain that making it to group is an example of "good" behavior, so there is at least one behavior that was not bad.

The goal of this activity is to get students to stop thinking of themselves in global terms such as "good" or "bad." Such thoughts are good examples of overgeneralizations that are common in many irrational thoughts. Students can be encouraged to remind themselves that no matter what difficulties they may be having they are still not "bad."

Acting "bad" is a universal trait that every one shares from time to time, but no one is 100 percent bad.

FOLLOW-UP MEETINGS

The intention of follow-up meetings is simple. You want to assess how well the group members have been managing their anger since the last group meeting. You may want to start with clients who have had success. Once again, if you work in the schools you will probably already have a pretty good idea of how they have been doing by the number of times you have seen them in the office since group therapy ended.

Don't expect students to act like completely different individuals in a few weeks. You plant some seeds, and some of the seeds take root. I have also been pleasantly surprised by some students whom I believed had not learned much from the group experience who somehow managed to master a great deal of the material. It is not always easy to tell who is learning and who is not. Time will be the ultimate judge.

CLASSROOM LESSONS

As mentioned previously, lessons on REBT for all fourth-grade students are part of the developmental guidance program in the district where I worked. This was an important part of our commitment to educating all children in the principles of rational decision making. (Refer to the section "Group Lessons" if you feel you have adequate information to apply those lessons to an elementary classroom.)

Your district may not place the same priority on rational decision making as mine. Classroom teachers can conduct these lessons if your district does not have an elementary guidance program or does not believe that these lessons fit into the model they are using. Some teachers have a skill for getting these lessons across because of their years of experience as educators. They know their students and also know how to help the class understand the concepts. Many of the lessons are similar to techniques used in groups.

Lesson 1

Lesson 1 starts by asking the class the simple question, "Where do our feelings come from?" or "What causes us to feel the way we do?" Most responses have in common the perception that our feelings are caused by situations, events, and other people. Only once did I come across a student who already understood that people cause the emotions they experience. She had gathered this insight through her own observations or had learned it from her parents. This is rare, but it does happen.

After students give their answers, explain that what actually causes people to feel happy, sad, angry, or uptight is their thoughts *about* events and situations, not the situations themselves. Expect to see some confused looks because this information is opposed to common opinion.

To illustrate the point that beliefs and evaluations cause feelings, ask the class to close their eyes. Next read an "A" such as, "You get home from school and see a letter from the principal in with the mail. All students who would be happy raise their hands." Usually there are only a handful of students who would be happy. Ask some of the students who did not raise their hands why they wouldn't be happy. They usually state that they would be concerned the letter could contain bad news. Then ask the students who had their hands raised what they were thinking to make themselves happy. Most will say something to the effect that they didn't think they were in trouble for anything, so they would expect the letter to be good news. The important point is that it was not the letter that caused anyone to feel happy or sad, it was their thoughts *about* the letter. If events could cause feelings, everyone would have felt the same way about the letter. Obviously there was a range of emotions in the room.

You can do the same experiment with other "As," for example:

- Got home from school and found out you were getting a new kitten.
- Got home from school and found out that you were moving into a new house.

Next explain that there are two kinds of beliefs:

1. *rational* or true beliefs and
2. *irrational* or false beliefs.

To determine if a belief is rational or irrational it is necessary to search for proof. The importance of proof is established using the "miracle diet pill" story.

The worksheet entitled "Where's the Proof?" (appendix C) is then handed out to the class and they are given time to complete the sheet in class. After everyone has completed the worksheet the statements can be examined by the class. Allow time for discussion of the reasons students answered the way they did.

Lesson 2

Lesson 2 begins with a review. Stress the need to find proof to be certain beliefs are rational. An exercise I typically use during the second lesson is called "Fact or Opinion." As the name implies, students are given the opportunity to determine if a statement is a fact, and therefore provable, or merely an opinion.

This can be easily turned into a game by dividing the room in half. You can play Tic-Tac-Toe, with each player having the chance to pronounce a statement as fact or opinion. Following are statements that I use during this exercise:

- Pepperoni is the best kind of pizza. (opinion)
- Kids in fourth grade are wonderful. (opinion)
- Green beans are a vegetable. (fact)
- Hockey is great. (opinion)
- Tomorrow will be awful. (opinion)
- Checkers is a game. (fact)
- Milwaukee is a great city. (opinion)
- Milwaukee is in Wisconsin. (fact)
- Fall is the best season of the year. (opinion)

After the game is completed, emphasize that not all people have the same opinions or beliefs about things. Because there are different opinions about different events, people will feel differently about the same events.

If time permits it can be helpful to review the difference between rational and irrational beliefs. Following are important distinctions that were discussed previously:

Rational Beliefs
- are true
- can be supported by evidence or proof
- are logical
- are *not* absolute commands
- are desires, wishes, hopes, and preferences
- produce moderate emotions such as sadness, irritation, and concern
- help you reach your goals

Irrational Beliefs
- are false
- lead to inaccurate deductions
- often are overgeneralizations
- are commands, shoulds, and needs
- lead to disturbed emotions such as depression, rage, and anxiety
- keep you from reaching your goals

Give the students additional practice distinguishing between these two types of beliefs by using the worksheet "Rational versus Irrational Beliefs" (appendix E). Students read each statement and decide whether the belief is provable and therefore rational, or unprovable and therefore irrational. After the students have completed their worksheets, read the answers and discuss them as a class.

Maxie Maultsby's test of rationality can be used to help students make this determination if they need some support. Maultsby (1975) encourages his clients to ask the following questions to determine if a belief is rational:

1. Can I prove this belief to be true?
2. Does this belief help to protect my life and health?
3. Does this belief help me get what I want?

4. Does this thinking help me to avoid unwanted conflicts with others?

5. Does this belief help me to feel the emotions I want to feel?

If the answer is "yes" to any three of the questions, it is mostly rational. If two or fewer are answered affirmatively, a belief is irrational and self-defeating.

Lesson 3

Lesson 3 involves letting students attempt to change irrational beliefs into rational beliefs. In keeping with the motto, "the simpler, the better," stress that usually only a word or two needs to be modified to make the transformation from irrational to rational. For example, the irrational belief, "I have to be correct all the time" can be changed to, "It would be nice to be correct most of the time." After the worksheet "Changing the Irrational" (appendix F) has been completed independently it can be examined in a large group discussion.

Lesson 4

Lesson 4 uses the "Let's Get Rational" game. With a class of twenty students it is necessary to divide the group in half and allow two games to run at once. Attempt to float between groups and help students if they have trouble with a portion of the game. For a group this size there aren't enough game pieces for every player, so you will have to use coins or some other objects in place of game pawns.

EFFICACY OF THE CLASSROOM LESSONS

These four classroom lessons are but an introduction to the concepts of REBT. Even though this exposure to REBT is limited, it can have a significant impact on students' thinking. This short curriculum has been evaluated and found to be effective in minimizing the endorsement of irrational beliefs (Wilde, 1997). Ninety-five fourth-grade students received four 30-minute lessons for a total of 120 minutes of

Rational Emotive Education (REE) instruction. Lesson 1 focused on the relationship between thoughts and emotions. Lesson 2 taught students to discriminate between rational and irrational beliefs. Lesson 3 was designed to help students change irrational thoughts into rational cognitions. During the last session students played the "Let's Get Rational" game, which was designed to teach rational thinking. A two-tailed t-test administered to examine differences between pre- and post-test scores on The Idea Inventory was statistically significant, t (1,94) = 5.90, $p < .0001$. Additionally, t scores for three of the five classroom scores reached statistical significance ($p < .05$). Students endorsed fewer irrational beliefs following the class lessons than when they were originally tested prior to the beginning of the lessons.

This same group of students was again evaluated while in eighth grade to determine if the changes in their thinking had been maintained over the four years since treatment in fourth grade (Wilde, 1999). A two-tailed t-test administered to examine the differences between pre-test scores in the fourth grade and post-test scores on The Idea Inventory in the eighth grade was statistically significant, t (1, 59) = 5.62, $p < .0001$, suggesting that the gains in rational thinking achieved following treatment had been maintained.

To ensure that this maintenance of rational thinking was not merely the result of maturation, eighth-graders who had not yet received treatment were compared with treatment subjects. These nontreatment subjects were students who were not enrolled in the school district during their fourth-grade year. Nontreatment subjects endorsed significantly more irrational beliefs than the eighth-graders who had received treatment in the fourth grade, t (1, 116) = 2.02, $p < .05$.

CONCLUSION

Due to the demand for such services, anger control groups might be the most efficient means of providing anger management interventions to students. The size of the group is important: Having too many students may lead to behavioral problems, which can jeopardize the group process. Co-facilitation can be helpful with managing behavior. The use of confederates can also have a positive impact on group members.

Students can be given the opportunity to refer themselves to group and can receive more detailed information through a screening process. Six to eight weeks is an ideal length of time for an AC group to meet. A follow-up meeting is recommended to determine if the progress has been maintained since the time of the last group meeting.

Students who have already been exposed to the basics will require less time going over fundamental concepts when AC groups start. Another hidden advantage is the knowledge and information the fourth-grade teaching staff receives. The faculty are in a position to use and reinforce the concepts taught in these lessons throughout the day.

Classroom lessons in mid-elementary grades can be an effective means of introducing REBT concepts. Teachers can reinforce information learned through the lessons to help students cope with their anger.

CHAPTER 11

Additional Anger Management Techniques

Numerous interventions have been presented in previous chapters that are designed to be used with anger-prone students. Most of the ideas have been designed to be used in a one-on-one counseling setting. Little attention has been paid to interventions created for use in classroom settings. The following techniques are proposed for teachers who are struggling with the behavior of angry and aggressive children. Many of these techniques are applicable to student misbehavior in general.

*DO*S AND *DON'T*S WITH ANGRY STUDENTS

When a student is close to an outburst, the teacher's actions become crucial. The proper responses from the teacher can prevent a blowup. However, if a teacher makes a poor choice, an outburst can be provoked, so the decisions made at certain times in the classroom are very important.

*Do*s

- *Do* listen carefully to an angry student. Sometimes just letting students know they are understood can go a long way toward calming them down. Adults sometimes forget how frustrating it can be when the person you're talking to isn't listening. An adolescent feels the same way. Just by letting a student know you (the teacher) care about his or her feelings can help diffuse the problem.
- *Do* call students by name to calm them down. It's important to use

a student's name because it reaffirms the personal connection the teacher has with the student.

- *Do* try to distract the angry student. If the teacher can somehow distract the student from the matter at hand, even for a few seconds, the child will benefit from the brief interruption. The distraction gives him or her a few seconds to think before acting, and that can make the difference between a good choice and a bad one.
- *Do* something unusual. A colleague of mine used to start having a conversation with an imaginary person. Students would often stop whatever they were doing just to listen to his "talk" with his invisible friend.
- *Do* start fresh each day. Try not to keep a running tally of problems, because students need to know that each new day is a chance to start over. Don't be an injustice collector.

Don'ts

- *Don't* raise your voice. Raising your voice will only escalate the situation. If any angry student starts shouting, lower your voice.
- *Don't* place your hands on the student (unless it is a safety concern). When a student is angry, a way to make a bad situation worse is to try to physically control the student. The obvious exception is when a student is a threat to himself or others. Placing your hands on the student will not only escalate the situation, it's also a good way to hurt the student or get hurt yourself.
- *Don't* crowd the student. Instead of approaching the student, double your distance.
- *Don't* take the insults personally. Even if the student picks on your individual characteristics, the verbal attack is still not intended to be personal. The student is angry and would have lashed out at whomever was in the class at that time.
- *Don't* use threats or bribes. Threats will not be effective because when students are truly "mad," they are momentarily incapable of making good choices. That is not to say that when students violate class and school rules, they should go unpunished. Not using threats during an anger episode means not dispensing punishment

during the event in an attempt to get compliance. This almost never works.

Bribes such as, "If you quiet down, maybe we can go out to recess early today," will only lead to more unruly behavior in the future. Bribes send the message, "If I act up, the teacher will give me what I want," and that's the wrong message to send.

Thankfully, not every moment in a classroom is spent on the verge of an outburst. The quiet times are when the hard work of establishing behavior management systems must be done. Following are a few ideas that are not found in most of the books on classroom management.

THE CAROL BURNETT TECHNIQUE

Students who are actively aggressive and have a history of acting out their anger can also be passively aggressive at times. They may not be in the midst of an explosion, but they can still be difficult to deal with because of their oppositional tendencies. These students often will resist attempts to gain compliance simply out of the desire to keep from feeling controlled. That is why common behavior interventions (detention, a trip to the principal's office) often prove ineffective with angry students.

The Carol Burnett technique is a behavior management intervention that can be used to redirect a student's behavior without drawing attention to the student. It is named after Carol Burnett because she used to gently pull on her ear lobe at the end of her show as a way of saying a secret "goodnight" to her children.

Chronically angry students often think of the Carol Burnett technique as a game rather than an attempt to control their behavior. The presentation is the key to this technique.

First, it is necessary to pick out a target behavior. The target can be any behavior the teacher wants diminished, such as making excessive noise during seat work. It is necessary to select a target behavior that is observable and clearly understood by both the adult and the student. Avoid vague targets like "follow school rules." It's better to define the particular rule that is being violated (e.g., bothering others by talking, calling out answers without raising your hand).

Once you have the target behavior clearly identified, it is best to have an individual conference with the student. Ask the student if he or she would like to play a game. Emphasize that no one else in the class will be able to play. Most students in elementary grades will love this idea. Explain that this game is going to be just between you and the student. It's a secret, and if both parties do their respective jobs, it can remain a secret. That's the goal, to see if the Carol Burnett technique can work without anybody figuring out what's occurring.

You should say something like, "You know how you've been having that problem with making too much noise at your desk? I've been having to tell you to quiet down because others are trying to work. Then you get mad because you feel like I'm picking on you. Also, I don't like having to call your name all the time, so I have a plan. Instead of telling you to quiet down, I'm going to give you a secret signal. I'm going to touch my ear when you're making too much noise. That's the secret signal for you to quiet down. I'm not going to say a thing, just touch my ear from wherever I am. Okay? Let's see if we can keep this our secret."

It is possible to develop a contract for rewards if the behavior improves, but it's best just to let the plan, the secret, be the reinforcement. It's also possible to switch the target behavior if necessary. It would not be wise to have more than one target behavior for a student at any one time. Otherwise it could become confusing for the teacher and student.

This technique works very well with elementary students. By middle and high school, students will view this intervention as just another way to control their behavior and as a result, this would probably not be an effective intervention.

THE "GET AWAY" PASS

A good means of minimizing blow-ups involves the use of "get away" passes. Students can be given a small number (two or three) at the start of the week and then allowed to time themselves out for a short period.

Prior to putting this plan in motion, hold a meeting to decide where the student can go. It's obviously a bad idea to allow the student to just leave the room with no destination in mind.

The "get away" should be as short as possible, no longer than thirty minutes. The professional on the "receiving" end will try to understand the nature of the problem and give the student whatever support is possible. Don't underestimate the importance of allowing the student to just relax for a few minutes or tell a counselor about the situation.

POSITIVE POWER OF THE PEER GROUP

Teachers sometimes forget that the class can work *with* them to help control disruptive students. The peer group can have an important impact on an individual student's behavior, and there are techniques that allow teachers to use this influence in a positive manner.

One way to use the positive power of the peer group is set up group incentives in which the entire class benefits if everyone acts appropriately. The beauty of group incentives is that students will start to encourage other students to behave rather than inviting chaos into the classroom. Rather than encouraging the anger-prone student to have another explosion, classmates are much more apt to counsel against misbehavior because now every student has a stake in the entire class's behavior.

MYSTERY STUDENT

The mystery student is similar to the positive power of the peer group. It is an intervention designed to be used for a difficult period of time, such as immediately following recess or prior to lunch. Students will also enjoy the mystery student because it is a little break from the routine of the day.

To start the mystery student game, every student's name should be placed in a container. The teacher then draws one name at a time. The identity of the mystery student should not be revealed at this point.

The class's job is simple: They are to follow the classroom agreements for that particular time of the day and activity. If the mystery student behaves appropriately the entire class can receive a reward. Since the mystery student's identity isn't known, students will encourage each other to behave because whoever is acting up could be the mystery student.

At the end of the prearranged period of time, if the mystery student has not met the behavioral expectations, his or her identity should *not* be revealed to the group. This could make the student a target for harassment. If the mystery student has met the expectations and earned a reward for the class, his or her identity should be revealed so he or she can receive praise from the class.

WEEKLY CLASS MEETINGS

It is a good idea for teachers to monitor the mood of the class on a regular basis and intervene early when the mood is combative and generally irritable. A good way to do this is through weekly class meetings.

The meetings can be short (thirty minutes) and can consist of some structured activities to get conversation flowing. One idea that students will like is to have each student start the meeting by recounting one "brag" (something they are proud of) and one "bummer" (one thing they'd like to do better or one thing they feel bad about). Meetings can allow the teacher and students to discuss issues that need clarifying. This is a good way of nipping a potential problem in the bud.

ERRANDS

When you can tell that a student is becoming frustrated and may have an explosion, a good distraction is to have that student run an errand for you. It is easy enough to have a small number of notes in labeled envelopes. Ask the student, "Could you take this to Mrs. Smith?" When the note is given to Mrs. Smith, it reads, "This student needed a short break. Thanks!"

CONCLUSION

Classroom teachers have a tough job managing anger-prone students in a classroom setting. Following is a brief review of the *do*s and *don't*s for handling angry students.

*Do*s

- *Do* listen carefully to an angry student.
- *Do* call a student by name.
- *Do* try to distract the angry student.
- *Do* something unusual.
- *Do* start fresh each day.

*Don't*s

- *Don't* raise your voice.
- *Don't* place your hands on the student (unless it is a safety concern).
- *Don't* crowd the student.
- *Don't* take the insults personally.
- *Don't* use threats or bribes.

There are other classroom management interventions such as the Carol Burnett technique, positive power of the peer group, and the mystery student. Weekly class meetings are a good means of monitoring the mood of the class on a regular basis and intervening early when necessary.

CHAPTER 12

Strategies for Keeping Students Safe

The fallout from the rash of school shootings has been widespread. Indeed, these shootings have turned the nation's focus away from fundamental issues regarding academics to issues related to school safety. Educators need to take care of safety issues before they can focus on teaching. This chapter contains some suggestions designed to maximize student safety so teachers can get back to the job of educating children and adolescents.

SECURITY STAFF

Most school buildings, even in smaller districts, have at least one individual whose role it is to monitor the building and campus on a regular basis. In the past this individual may have been a principal or assistant principal or perhaps even the groundskeeper or custodian. These individuals had other responsibilities but were on the lookout for situations that could prove problematic (e.g., a stranger hanging around the parking lot or sitting in a car near the school). Monitoring the campus was a secondary responsibility.

Today, more and more schools are hiring full-time security staff whose sole responsibility is to maintain a safe campus. These individuals often are uniformed and work in conjunction with local law enforcement. These security personnel are visible and often interact with students in hallways and at extracurricular events.

METAL DETECTORS

Metal detectors are becoming commonplace in schools. There are a variety of models, from hand-held to the larger "walk through" metal detectors found in airports.

These devices are certainly a deterrent to a student bringing a weapon in through the front door, but students know there are a variety of other points of entry into schools. Doors can be locked to keep intruders from entering the school, but students inside the building can always open a door to let in a student with a weapon.

School employees have mixed feelings about metal detectors in their buildings, and with good reason. Most teachers certainly understand the importance of students feeling safe and secure. *Children and adolescents will not be able to focus on learning if they do not feel physically and emotionally safe.* There are concerns that the sight of metal detectors on entering the school will be a constant reminder of the need to be concerned. This is a classic paradox of decreasing feelings of security by attempting to ensure safety.

If a district has the financial resources to put metal detectors in place but is uncertain of their emotional impact, it may be wise to conduct a survey of students, school employees, and parents. The findings from research journals or think tanks are not nearly as relevant as the responses by members of a given school and community.

IDENTIFICATION BADGES

Schools are beginning to require staff members to wear some type of identification badge at all times. Some schools also require students to wear such badges.

Every entrance to a school should have a sign directing all visitors to the office, where they can be given a visitor's badge that identifies that person to all students and staff as having been cleared to be in the building.

Any staff member who sees a visitor in the building without the pass should approach the individual and ask, "May I help you?" If the visitor has not been to the office for a visitor's pass, he or she should be directed to do so and, if necessary, escorted to the office.

"BETWEEN" TIMES

A majority of behavioral problems tend to occur during "between" times when students are moving from class to class, immediately after lunch, and before or after school. These down times need adequate supervision to keep problems to a minimum and to stop minor situations from escalating. An innocent bump in the lunch line may lead to a physical fight after school. Having plenty of eyes and ears available during these times is a good way of getting the pulse of a building.

ESTABLISH A PARENT CENTER

Each school should consider establishing a parent center that recruits and encourages parents to participate in the education of their children. Volunteers can help supervise hallways, restrooms, or other areas. Obviously, parents are a great resource for teachers in class as well. Schools will need to train these parents and make certain the volunteers have a clear understanding of the school's expectations.

ONGOING STAFF DEVELOPMENT

The professionals who work in a school building are the most important resource. A state-of-the-art building will not become a high-quality school without motivated, energetic, and caring teachers. Conversely, quality education can take place almost anywhere, regardless of the facility.

School staff needs and deserves ongoing professional development in important topics such as classroom management, safety issues, and anger management.

ADOPTING AND USING AN ANTI-HARASSMENT POLICY

Many of the perpetrators of school violence were targets of bullies. Some of the cases of school violence were carried out in direct retaliation for years of hazing. This was certainly true at Columbine High School in Littleton, Colorado, where Dylan Kleibold and Eric Harris reported being hit and bullied in the hallways on a regular basis.

Sadly, some schools accept harassment as a normal part of adolescent development. The unspoken message to both the victim and aggressor is, "There is nothing the school is going to do about this." This attitude just exacerbates the situation because it gives a green light to the bully and makes the victim feel even more desperate. It's not surprising that some students felt as though they have to take matters into their own hands.

The truth of the matter is that there is a great deal schools can do to curb harassment. Schools have the authority and obligation to do everything in their power to provide a safe and hostility-free environment. Parents and students have begun filing lawsuits against schools for their inability to provide a safe environment. Districts must wake up and become proactive about these situations or find good lawyers— and their checkbooks. If an employee can successfully sue an employer for the failure to provide a hostility-free workplace, why are schools foolish enough to think they are not going to be held to the same standard?

The first step is adopting a tough policy that clearly defines what is and what is not harassment. Students need to be inserviced regarding harassment and the potential consequences of continuing with this behavior. There should be significant consequences when the harassment will not stop. Finally, the administration needs to be prepared to use the policy.

The East Troy School District in East Troy, Wisconsin, adopted a policy that has worked quite well. Our high school principal, Sue Alexander, used this program effectively in her previous district, and her expertise was invaluable.

When a complaint of harassment was brought to the attention of the school, the first step was to bring the two students together and let them tell their sides of the story. It's important to allow students to express their perceptions and feelings about the incident(s) in question. Each student was then told to "cease and desist." In adolescent language, they were told, "Knock it off. I don't care who started it and I don't care who retaliated, it ends now." They were also informed that further harassment would lead to serious consequences such as suspension from school. There were no negative consequences from this first meeting, and if there were no further difficulties, the case was dropped, but records of the meeting were kept on file.

If there were further reports of harassment, the next step was to do an investigation to determine from eyewitness accounts what actually occurred. If a student had engaged in harassment after being given the verbal cease and desist order, that student would be suspended from school.

If there was a third substantiated incident of harassment, that student would be required to appear before the school board. The potential consequence of this third offense was expulsion for the remainder of the semester or the remainder of the school year.

Our district's policy worked very well because the students bought into the plan. It took a little more than a semester before any student was expelled from school. This student was able to receive homebound instruction and did not fall behind in credits. Following her expulsion, the student body knew this policy would be enforced and that the consequences would be severe.

Students were initially hesitant to come forward, not wanting to appear to be weak in the eyes of their peers. Once students started getting good results (i.e., having the harassment stopped) from coming forward, they were more and more willing to use the new policy.

These policies can be very effective if the district is committed to making them work. Unfortunately, many school districts have these policies on their books but don't believe in or use them.

PEER HELPERS

There are many different names for peer helper programs. Regardless of the program's title, peer helpers are an important part of school safety programs.

Adolescents often feel more comfortable speaking with peers. Some students will disclose information to teenagers that they would never dream of telling an adult. Think of peer helper programs as another line of communication available to troubled students.

PROMOTING COMMUNICATION

Most of you have never heard of Burlington, Wisconsin. It's a small town in southeastern Wisconsin close to where I lived and worked for many years.

A handful of Burlington High School students planned to carry out a Columbine-type massacre at their school. There apparently was a "hit list" of students to be executed, and the goal of the would-be assailants was to kill as many of the students, staff, and administration as possible.

The reason people don't speak of Burlington, Wisconsin, the way they speak of Columbine comes down to one student. One student had the courage to report the plan on the Friday prior to the attack, which was scheduled for the following Monday. Very few people in Burlington (other than the assistant principal) know this individual's name, but his or her actions surely saved many lives.

We need to get this message to every student: If students hear of plans to hurt others, they need to come forward. Informing teachers or other staff members can't be thought of as "narcing" anymore. It takes real courage to come forward, and we need to make that clear. Today in American schools, the cost of remaining silent is the blood of innocent students and teachers.

CONCLUSION

To become safer, schools may want to consider hiring professional security staff. Metal detectors are becoming increasingly popular in schools today. Requiring students and staff to wear identification badges is a good way of allowing school personnel to clearly recognize people who do not belong in the building. Monitoring "between" times can keep small problems from escalating. By establishing a parent center, schools are welcoming the public into the building and gaining additional resources to help students in any number of ways. Ongoing staff development is important to keep teachers up-to-date in important areas like harassment and building safety. An anti-harassment policy can be extremely beneficial as a means of stopping bullies. Peer helpers are another means of allowing students to communicate their problems. Peers give students someone else to go to if they feel uncomfortable confiding in staff members.

CHAPTER 13

School-Wide Safety Assessment

One of my goals for this revised edition of *Anger Management in Schools* has been to adequately address a wider range of factors that contribute to anger and violence in our schools. The first edition dealt almost exclusively with intra-individual factors. That was most likely the result of my personal belief that we had better help children and adolescents learn to take responsibility for their thoughts, feelings, and behaviors. Other people and situations do not *make* students angry or aggressive. Of all the fundamental underpinnings of this book, that belief is essential.

However, it is also important to remember that other people and situations do *contribute* to a students' feelings. Situations are important antecedents and it would be foolish to ignore that fact. It is with this in mind that I undertake a school safety assessment.

This assessment is designed to help you to become aware of the many factors that go into school violence prevention. It is not a norm-referenced instrument, so please don't send me a copy of your school's results and ask, "How did we do?" The only people able to answer that question are the professionals who work in your school and live in your community. Think of this checklist as an important review of your resources, both physical and programmatic. Change should never be made just for the sake of change, but unfortunately all too many schools are doing just that. It's best to take an honest look at your school's resources before deciding what needs improvement.

Directions: Place an "x" in the space provided for each statement that is true for your school.

Building

___ 1. Is the school enrollment small enough that a sense of "community" can be established?

___ 2. Does your school have adequate space for all classes without the need for temporary classrooms?

___ 3. If the answer to #2 is "no," are these temporary classrooms equipped with
    ___ a) telephones
    ___ b) alarms
    ___ c) doors that lock from the inside?

___ 4. Is the building monitored with
    ___ a) cameras
    ___ b) metal detectors?

___ 5. Is there adequate monitoring of high-risk events such as
    ___ a) sporting events
    ___ b) assemblies
    ___ c) graduations?

___ 6. Is there adequate monitoring of
    ___ a) lunch periods
    ___ b) recess
    ___ c) bathrooms?

___ 7. Is your school free of graffiti?

Programs

___ 1. Is there an anger management curriculum in place that is integrated into the core curriculum at appropriate times?

___ 2. Is there a conflict resolution curriculum in place that is integrated into the core curriculum at appropriate times?

___ 3. Is there a violence prevention curriculum in place that is integrated into the core curriculum at appropriate times?

___ 4. Is there a peer helper program available for students?

___ 5. Is there a conflict resolution program for staff and parents?

___ 6. Are the above-mentioned curricula sensitive to gender, ethnic, and cultural issues?

___ 7. Are there student clubs/groups that promote prosocial behavior?

___ 8. Is there a K–12 Student Assistance Program designed with the needs of high-risk students in mind?

___ 9. Are there community resources available on the topics of anger management, conflict resolution, and violence prevention?

___10. Are the programs evaluated on a yearly basis and revised accordingly?

Administration

___ 1. Does the administration include parents and community members in important decisions regarding the school?

___ 2. Is the administration supportive of anger management, violence prevention, conflict resolution, and peer helper programs?

___ 3. Is the administration actively involved in these programs?

___ 4. Does the administration provide adequate funding for the above-mentioned programs?

Policies/Practices

___ 1. Is there a crisis management team?

___ 2. Is there a crisis management plan in place?

___ 3. Is this plan reviewed annually so that all school employees know their roles?

___ 4. Does the school do an adequate job of restricting access to school grounds?

____ 5. Is the staff trained in practices to be used when an unauthorized visitor is in the building?

____ 6. At the middle school and high school, is there a "homeroom" for each student?

____ 7. Is this homeroom used in an attempt to build a sense of community?

____ 8. Is there a proactive approach to discipline?

____ 9. Does your school forbid the use of corporal punishment?

____10. Does your school forbid students to leave the grounds during lunch hour?

School Climate

____ 1. Is there a sense of community in the school?

____ 2. Is there a sense of community among the staff?

____ 3. Do parents generally feel welcome and appreciated while at school?

____ 4. Are staff members sensitive to gender, cultural, and ethnic issues?

____ 5. Is the discipline policy clearly understood by students?

____ 6. Is the discipline policy fairly administered?

____ 7. Is positive behavior recognized by the staff?

____ 8. Are parents made aware of positive behavior by their children?

Community

____ 1. Is your school in a community with a low crime rate?

____ 2. Are parents involved in the planning of violence prevention programs?

____ 3. Are there recreational activities for students in the community?

_____ 4. Is there a mentoring program (i.e., Big Brothers/Big Sisters) available in the community?

After looking over your results, what are your

Strengths: (List them below)

How can they be made even stronger?

On what areas do you need to focus?

What is your first priority?

Who should be part of your team to get results? Write down their names below.

Write down the date of your first team meeting below.

CHAPTER 14

Final Thoughts

I sincerely hope this book has provided some new ideas for programs that can make a difference in your schools. These techniques are "battle tested" and quite simply the best I know of for helping students to be less consumed by anger and therefore more able to direct their energies toward learning and growing.

The differences you will see in your building can be profound. There will be less hostility, which will bring about a more relaxed classroom atmosphere. The importance of the classroom atmosphere in the facilitation of learning cannot be overemphasized.

Students who are safe and secure in their surroundings will feel more confident about themselves. In a classroom where there is fear of harsh comments and criticism, the open exchange of ideas is inhibited. The searching, challenging, and exploration in learning are compromised.

The programs I suggest will diminish conflicts in your school. Educators know how much time during the day is spent mediating petty disputes. Many of these arguments can be eliminated before they start, leaving more time to teach.

If you have any questions about these lessons or any of the ideas presented in the book, do not hesitate to write or call me: Jerry Wilde, Indiana University East, 344 Middlefork Hall, 2325 Chester Blvd., Richmond, IN 47374; (765) 973–8554.

As one of your colleagues, I've "been there" and I know our jobs are some of the most difficult imaginable. Keep in mind that along with the headaches comes the opportunity for a great reward, much better than money can buy: the satisfaction we get when we connect with students and truly make a difference in their lives. In that moment we transcend time and come as close as humanly possible to being immortal. We touch, and positively influence, the future. These moments can be few and far between, but when they occur, they should be celebrated. Your dedication and persistence make positive things happen for students. Keep up the important work that you do.

Sample Contract

I hereby agree to the terms stated below in this contract. I am signing this contract under my own free will and pledge to honor these commitments.

1. I will be on time for all group meetings.

2. I will make up any and all missed assignments due to group participation.

3. I am willing to change my attitudes and behavior. I do not expect the entire world to change for me.

4. I accept responsibility for my anger. I am the one who causes me to be angry.

5. I will complete all practice exercises from the group to the best of my ability.

6. I will be a supportive member of the group and try to help other members.

_____

Name

_____

Date

The Anger Survey

Name _____

Date _____

Directions: Circle the number that best reflects how strongly you agree or disagree with each statement below.

Strongly Disagree   *Strongly Agree*

1. I get angry when things don't go as planned.
       1   2   3   4   5   6

2. Other people make me angry.
       1   2   3   4   5   6

3. Life should be fair.
       1   2   3   4   5   6

4. When I don't do well I get very angry with myself.
       1   2   3   4   5   6

5. Things have to be my way or I get angry.
       1   2   3   4   5   6

6. The world has to be a better place to live.
       1   2   3   4   5   6

7. My family can make me get angry.
       1   2   3   4   5   6

8. There are a lot of things that ought to be better than they are right now.
       1   2   3   4   5   6

9. I can't control my temper.
       1   2   3   4   5   6

10. I get mad when people don't act like I think they should.
        1   2   3   4   5   6

TOTAL _____

Where's the Proof?

Name _____

Directions: In the blank space in front of each belief, print a "T" if the belief is a true belief and an "F" if the belief is a false belief.

____ 1. I don't like it when I do poorly but it's not the worst thing in the world.

____ 2. Life has to be fair all the time.

____ 3. If people don't like me I can still like myself.

____ 4. I can't stand losing at something important.

____ 5. I wish things were easier in school, but they don't have to be.

____ 6. Other people make me feel bad.

____ 7. If I make a mistake once I will probably always make that mistake.

____ 8. Because math is hard for me it proves I'm a stupid person.

____ 9. If someone thinks I'm a nerd, I'm a nerd.

____10. No matter what you say or do to me, I'm still a worthwhile person.

____11. When things don't go the way I want, it's the worst thing ever.

____12. I have to be right 100 percent of the time.

____13. Things should go my way most of the time.

____14. For the most part, I can control how I feel.

Answer key:
True—1, 3, 5, 10, 14
False—2, 4, 6, 7, 8, 9, 11, 12, 13

Anger Incident Worksheet

Name _____

Date _____

Directions: Complete the worksheet with as much accuracy as is possible. Pretend you are recording this event as if you were a video camera with sound. A video camera couldn't show someone being mean to you. It could show someone calling you names.

1. When did you make yourself angry? (What date and time was it?)

2. Where were you when you made yourself angry?

3. Who else was present?

4. As specifically as possible, describe what happened.

5. What did you say to yourself to make yourself angry? (Hint: Listen to your self-talk and see if you can hear any SHOULDS, MUSTS, or OUGHT TO BES)

6. How could you change what you said to yourself to change your feelings? (Hint: Try changing your demanding SHOULDS, etc. to preferences like I WISH . . . , IT WOULD BE NICE. . . . I'D LIKE.)

Rational versus Irrational Beliefs

Name _____

Directions: Next to each statement print RB if the belief is a rational belief and IB if the belief is an irrational belief.

1. I wish I could have a new stereo.
2. If I don't do as well as I would have liked in math it doesn't mean I'm stupid.
3. My parents never let me go anywhere.
4. I don't like some subjects as much as others, but I can stand them anyway.
5. If I don't get asked to the dance, I'll die.
6. If I wear these old shoes, everyone will make fun of me.
7. I wish things would be easier, but they don't have to be.
8. I would prefer it if my parents would let me stay out later.
9. If a teacher gets mad at me I don't have to get down on myself.
10. If I didn't get on the honor role I couldn't show my face around here.
11. Even if I look like a fool if doesn't mean I am a fool.
12. People ought to treat me with the respect I deserve.

Changing the Irrational

Name _____

Directions: Underneath each irrational statement write a new, rational one.

1. Life has to treat me the way I want to be treated. _____

_____

2. I can't take it when things don't go my way. _____

_____

3. He doesn't have the right to say that to me. _____

_____

4. You have to help me because it is hard to do alone. _____

_____

5. Things never go my way. _____

_____

6. My classmates have to take my advice. _____

_____

7. My grades had better be good or I'll be a complete loser. _____

_____

8. It would be terrible, awful, and horrible if I didn't get my way. ___

_____

Parental Permission Form

Your child _____, has expressed an interest in attending an educational group that is designed to help students learn to control their anger. The group will meet once a week for ____ weeks in your child's school. If you have any questions please call _____. Thank you for your time.

(   ) I grant permission for my child to take part in the educational group.

(   ) I deny permission for my child to take part in the educational group.

_____   _____

Parent   Date

Triggers and Cues

Name _____

Outside triggers: What types of situations are you likely to get angry about?

1. _____

2. _____

3. _____

4. _____

Inside triggers: What types of thoughts are likely to light your fuse?

1. _____

2. _____

3. _____

4. _____

Cues: What happens in your body just before you become angry?

1. _____

2. _____

3. _____

4. _____

Bibliography

Adler, A. (1968). *Understanding human nature.* Greenwich, CT: Fawcett.

Angold, A., & Costello, E. (1993). Depressive comorbidity in children and adolescents: Empirical, theoretical and methodological issues. *American Journal of Psychiatry,* 150, (12), 1779–1791.

Averill, J. R. (1982). *Anger and aggression: An essay on emotion.* New York: Springer-Verlag.

Averill, J. R. (1983). Studies on anger and aggression: Implication for theories of emotions. *American Psychologist,* 38, 1145–1160.

Averill, J. R. (1993). Illusions of anger. In R. B. Felson & J. T. Tedeschi (Eds.), *Aggression and violence: Social interactionists perspectives* (pp. 172–191). Washington, DC: American Psychological Association.

Barefoot, J., Dahlstrom, G., & Williams, R. (1983). Hostility, CHD incidence, and total mortality: A twenty-five year study of 255 physicians. *Psychosomatic Medicine,* 45, 59–63.

Barefoot, J., Dodge, K., Peterson, B., Dahlstrom, G., & Williams, R. (1989). The Cook-Medley hostility scale: Item content and ability to predict survival. *Psychosomatic Medicine,* 51, 46–57.

Beck, A., & Shaw, B. (1977). Cognitive approaches to depression. In A. Ellis and R. Grieger (Eds.), *Handbook of rational-emotive therapy.* New York: Springer Press.

Berkowitz, L. (1970). Experimental investigations of hostility catharsis. *Journal of Consulting and Clinical Psychology,* 35, 1–7.

Bernard, M., & Joyce, M. (1984). *Rational-emotive therapy with children and adolescents: Theory, treatment strategies, and preventative methods.* New York: Wiley Interscience.

Blumberg, S., & Izard, C. (1985). Affective and cognitive characteristics of depression in 10- and 11-year-old children. *Journal of Personality and Social Psychology,* 49, 194–202.

187

Butts, J., & Snyder, H. (1997). The youngest deliquents: Offenders under age 15. *Juvenile Justice Bulletin,* September, pp. 1–11.

Covell, K., & Abramovitch, R. (1987). Understanding emotion in the family: Children's and parent's attributions of happiness, sadness, and anger. *Child Development,* 58, 985–991.

Crick, N., & Dodge, K. (1994). A review and reformulation of social-information processing mechanisms in children's social adjustment. *Psychological Bulletin,* 115, 74–101.

Cummings, E. (1987). Coping with background anger in early childhood. *Child Development,* 58, 976–984.

Deffenbacher, J. L. (1993). General anger: Characteristics and clinical implications. *Psicologia Conductual,* 1, 49–67.

Deffenbacher, J., Lynch, R., Oetting, E., & Kemper, C. (1996). Anger reduction in early adolescents. *Journal of Counseling Psychology,* 43, 149–157.

Dodge, K. (1986). A social information processing model of social competence in children. In M. Perlmutter (Ed.), *Cognitive perspectives on children's social and behavioral development: The Minnesota symposium on child psychology* (Vol. 18). Hillsdale, NJ: Erlbaum.

Dodge, K., & Frame, C. (1982). Social cognitive biases and deficits in aggressive boys. *Child Development,* 53, 620–635.

Dollard, J., Doob, L., Miller, N., Mowrer, O., & Sears, R. (1939). *Frustration and aggression.* New Haven, CT: Yale University Press.

Dryden, W. (1990). *Dealing with anger problems: Rational emotive therapeutic interventions.* Sarasota, FL: Professional Resource Exchange.

Ellis, A. (1957). Outcome of employing three techniques of psychotherapy. *Journal of Clinical Psychology,* 13, 344–350.

Ellis, A. (1962). *Reason and emotion in psychotherapy.* Secaucus, NJ: Citadel Press.

Ellis, A. (1973). *Humanistic psychotherapy.* New York: McGraw-Hill.

Ellis, A. (1976). The biological basis of human irrationality. *Journal of Individual Psychology,* 32, 145–168.

Ellis, A. (1977a). *Anger—how to live with and without it.* Secaucus, NJ: Citadel Press.

Ellis, A. (1977b). Introduction. In J. Wolfe and E. Brand (Eds.), *Twenty years of rational therapy.* New York: Institute for Rational-Emotive Therapy.

Ellis, A. (1985). *Overcoming resistance.* New York: Springer Press.

Eron, L., Huesman, L., Dubow, E., Romanoff, R., & Yarmel, P. (1987). Aggression and its correlates over 22 years. In D. Crowell, E. Evans, & C. O'Donnell (Eds.), *Aggression and violence: Sources of influence, prevention, and control* (pp. 249–262). New York: Plenum.

Farrington, D. (1977). The family backgrounds of aggressive youths. In L. Hersov, M. Beger, & D. Shafer (Eds.), *Aggression and antisocial behavior in childhood and adolescence* (pp. 73–93). Oxford: Pergamon.

Fava, M., Rosenbaum, J. F., Pava, J., McCarthy, M.K., Steingard, R., & Bouffides, E. (1993). Anger attacks in unipolar depression: Part 1. Clinical correlates and response to fluoxetine treatment. *American Journal of Psychiatry,* 150, 1158–1163.

Feshbach, S. (1971). The function of aggression and the regulation of aggressive drive. *Psychological Review,* 71, 257–272.

Freud, S. (1963). *Collected papers.* New York: Collier.

Fryxell, D. (2000). Personal, social, and family characteristics of angry students. *Professional School Counseling,* 4 (2), 86–95.

Gibbs, E., & Gibbs, F. (1951). Electroencephlographic evidence of thalamic and hypothalamic epilepsy. *Neurology,* 1, 136–144.

Greer, S., & Morris, T. (1975). Psychological attributes of women who develop breast cancer: A controlled study. *Journal of Psychosomatic Research,* 19, 147–153.

Grieger, R. (1982). Anger problems. In R. Grieger and I. Z. Grieger (Eds.), *Cognition and emotional disturbance.* New York: Human Science Press.

Harburg, E., Blakelock, E. H., & Roeper, P. J. (1979). Resentful and reflective coping with arbitrary/authority and blood pressure: Detroit. *Psychosomatic Medicine,* 3, 189–202.

Harburg, E., Gleiberman, L., Russell, M., & Cooper, L. (1991). Anger coping styles and blood pressure in black and white males. *Psychosomatic Medicine,* 53, 153–164.

Hauck, P. (1980). *Brief counseling with RET.* Philadelphia: Westminster Press.

Iribarren, C., Sidney, S., Bild, D., Liu, K., Markovitz, J., Rosenman, J., & Mathews, K. (2000). Association of hostility with coronary artery calcification in young adults: The CARDIA study. *Journal of American Medical Association,* 283, 2546–2551.

Johnson, E., Collier, P., Nazzarro, P., & Gilbert, D. (1992). Psychological and physiological predictors of lipids in Black males. *Journal of Behavioral Medicine,* 15, 285–298.

Kashani, J., Dahlmeier, J., Borduin, C., & Reid, J. (1995). Characteristics of anger expression in depressed children. *Journal of the American Academy of Child and Adolescent Psychiatry,* 34, 322–326.

Kiecolt-Glaser, J., Malarky, W., Chee, M., Newton, T., Cacioppo, J., Mao, H., & Glaser, R. (1993). Negative behavior during marital conflict is associated with immunological down-regulation. *Psychosomatic Medicine,* 55, 395–409.

Lewis, D. O. (1981). *Vulnerabilities to delinquency.* New York: Spectrum Medical and Scientific Books.

Liebsohn, M., Oetting, E., & Deffenbacher, J. (1994). Effects of trait anger on alcohol consumption and consequences. *Journal of Child and Adolescent Substance Abuse,* 3, 17–32.

Lopez, F., & Thurman, C. (1993). High-trait and low-trait college students: A comparison of family environments. *Journal of Counseling and Development,* 71, 524–528.

Luria, A. (1973). *The working brain.* New York: Basic Books.

Mallik, S., & McCandless, B. (1966). A study of catharsis aggression. *Journal of Personality and Social Psychology,* 4, 591–596.

Maslow, A. (1959). *New knowledge in human values.* New York: Harper Bothers.

Maultsby, M. (1975). *Help yourself to happiness.* New York: Institute for Rational-Emotive Therapy.

Murdoch, B. (1972). Electroencephologograms, aggression and emotional maturity in psychopathic and non-psychopathic prisoners. *Psychologia Africana,* 14, 216–231.

Murray, E. (1985). Coping with anger. In T. Field, P. McCabe, & N. Schneiderman (Eds.), *Stress and coping.* Hillsdale, NJ: Erlbaum.

National Center for Educational Statistics (NCES) (1998). *U.S. Department of Education: Indicators of school crime and safety, 1998.* Washington, DC: NCES, U.S. Department of Education.

National School Safety Center News Service (1997). *School safety update.* Malibu, CA: National School Safety Center.

Peters, L. (1977). *Peter's quotations: Ideas for our time.* New York: Bantam.

Petersen, A., Compas, B., Brooks-Gunn, J., Stemmler, M., Ey, S., & Grant, K. (1993). Depression in adolescence. *American Psychologist,* 48, 155–168.

Ramsey, R. (1974) Emotional training. *Behavioral Engineering,* 1, 24–26.

Reynolds, W. (1992). Depression in children and adolescents. In W. Reynolds (Ed.), *Internalizing disorders in children and adolescents.* New York: John Wiley.

Rule, B., & Nesdale, A. (1976). Emotional arousal and aggressive behavior. *Psychological Bulletin,* 83, 851–863.

The school shooter: A threat perspective assessment. (1999). Quantico, VA: Critical Incident Response Group (CIRG), National Center for the Analysis of Violent Crime (NCAVC), FBI Academy.

Shekelle, R., Gale, M., Ostfeld, A., & Oglesby, P. (1983). Hostility, risk of coronary disease and mortality. *Psychosomatic Medicine,* 45, 219–228.

Siegel, J., & Brown, J. (1988). A prospective study of stressful circumstances, illness symptoms, and depressed mood among adolescents. *Developmental Psychology,* 24, 715–721.

Singer, J., Singer, D., & Rapaczynski, W. (1984). Family patterns and television viewing as predictors of children's belief and aggression. *Journal of Communication,* 24, 73–89.

Smith, D., & Furlong, M. (1994). Correlates of anger, hostility, and aggression in children and adolescents. In M. J. Furlong & D. C. Smith (Eds.), *Anger, hostility, and aggression: Assessment, prevention, and intervention strategies for youth* (pp. 15–38). New York: John Wiley.

Smith, D., Furlong, M., Bates, M., & Laughlin, J. (1998). Development of the multidimensional school anger inventory for males. *Psychology in the Schools,* 35, 1–15.

Soloman, P., & Kleeman, A. (1971). Medical aspects of violence. *California Medicine,* 114, 19–24.

Spielberger, C. (1988). *State-trait anger expression inventory (STAXI).* Orlando, FL: Psychological Assessment Resources.

Spielberger, C., Jacobs, G., Russell, S., & Crane, R. (1983). Assessment of anger: The State Trait Anger Scale. In J. Butcher & C. Spielberger (Eds.), *Advances in personality assessment* (Vol. 2, pp. 112–134). Hillsdale, NJ: Erlbaum.

Spielberger, C. D., Crane, R. S., Kearns, W. D., Pellegrin, K. L., & Rickman, R. L. (1991). Anger and anxiety in essential hypertension. In C. D. Spielberger, I. G. Sarason, Z. Kulcar, & G. L. Van Heck (Eds.), *Stress and emotion: Anxiety, anger and curiosity* (pp. 265–279). New York: Taylor & Francis.

Trimpey, J. (1992). *The small book.* New York: Delacorte Press.

U.S. Department of Education and U.S. Department of Justice. (1999). *Annual Report on School Safety.* [Online]. Available at www.ojp.usdoj.gov/bjs/abstract/iscs99.htm.

Waldstein, S., Manuck, S., Bachen, E., Muldoon, M., & Bricker, P. (1990). Anger expression, lipids, and lipoproteins. Poster session presented at the 11th Annual Meeting of the Society for Behavioral Medicine, Chicago, April.

Walen, S., DiGiuseppe, R., & Wessler, R. (1980). *A practitioner's guide to rational-emotive therapy.* New York: Oxford University Press.

Waters, V. (1980). *Rational stories for children.* New York: Institute for Rational-Emotive Therapy.

Wilde, J. (1992). *Rational counseling with school-aged populations: A practical guide.* Muncie, IN: Accelerated Development.

Wilde, J. (1994). The effects of the let's get rational board game on rational thinking, depression, and self-acceptance in adolescents. *The Journal of Rational-Emotive & Cognitive-Behavior Therapy,* 12 (3), 189–196.

Wilde, J. (1995a). *Anger management in schools: Alternatives to student violence.* Lancaster, PA: Technomic.

Wilde, J. (1995b). *Treating anger, anxiety, and depression in children and adolescents: A cognitive-behavioral perspective.* New York: Taylor & Francis.

Wilde, J. (1997). The efficacy of short-term rational-emotive education with fourth grade students. *Elementary School Guidance and Counseling,* 31, 131–138.

Wilde, J. (1999). The long term efficacy of short term rational-emotive education: A follow up evaluation. *The Journal of Cognitive Psychotherapy,* 13, 92–101.

Williams, D. (1969). Neural factors associated with habitual aggression. *Brain,* 92, 503–520.

Young, H. (1974). *A rational counseling primer.* New York: Institute for Rational-Emotive Therapy.

Youth Risk Behavior Survey–United States (1999). [Online]. Available at www.cdc.gov/mmwr/preview/mmwrhtml/ss4095a1.htm#tab6.

the ABCs, 34, 77, 99, 108–10,
    133–35
Adler, A., 38
adolescent clients, 66–67
anger: causes of, 27–28; charting, 98;
    episodes of, 69; groups, 123–53;
    learning environment, 4–5
assertiveness training, 96
Averill, J., 5, 69–70

Barefoot, J., 10
Beck, A., 103, 105
behavior therapy, 46–47, 57
beliefs leading to anger, 35–38
Berkowitz, L., 9

Carol Burnett technique, 157–58
classroom lessons, 147–52
client-centered therapy, 47–48, 58
co-facilitation, 126
cognitive distraction, 89
confederates, 127

Deffenbacher, J., 13–14
depression, 22, 101–6
disputations, 35, 84
divide and conquer, 125
Dodge, K., 15–19

elementary-aged clients, 65–68
Ellis, A., 35, 45, 48, 50, 88
emotional training, 94–95
errands, 160–61

forceful dialogue, 93
Freud, S., 38
frustration-aggression hypothesis, 28
full acceptance, 93–94

get away passes, 158–59
Greer, S., 7, 9
Greiger, R., 9

hangman, 145
harassment, 166–67
health, 9–11
"Hot Stuff to Help Kids Chill Out,"
    135

icebreakers, 132
identification badges, 164–65
indications of school crime and
    safety, 3
inner child therapy, 49–50, 58
irrational beliefs, 33–34, 52–56, 62,
    78, 81, 150, 183, 184

"Let's Get Rational" game, 139–41,
    151

low frustration tolerance, 39–42
Luria, A., 29

Mallik, B., 9
Maultsby, M., 34
mystery student, 159–60

neurology, 18–19

paradoxical intention, 88
parents, 130–31, 165, 185
patience, 39–40
peer group, 159
peer helpers, 167–68
pragmatic disputes, 92–93
primal scream therapy, 48–49, 58
proof, 181
psychoanalysis, 45–46, 57

"Rate Your Week," 136
rational beliefs, 52–56, 78, 81, 183
Rational-Emotive Imagery, 82–84,
    92, 150
Rational Role Reversal, 95
rational story telling technique,
    96–97

referrals, 59–60, 128–29
reinforcement, 89–90
role playing, 99
rubber band technique, 91
Rule, B., 5

safety assessment, 171–75
school shootings, 1–2
search for control technique, 87
security staff, 163
self-acceptance, 145
Skinner, B. F., 46
speaking ball, 125
Speilberger, C., 7, 9

tape and worksheet, 63–64
thinking patterns, 13–14
time out, 125–26
time projection, 98
triggers and cues, 141–42

violence, 5–6, 25; entertainment, 22

weekly class meetings, 160

Young, H., 127–35
youth risk behavior survey, 2–3

About the Author

Jerry Wilde is an assistant professor of educational psychology for Indiana University East. Prior to this academic appointment, he had nine years of experience as a school psychologist, during which time he counseled students who had emotional, behavioral, and learning difficulties.

Dr. Wilde has written numerous books, including the following:

More Hot Stuff to Help Kids Chill Out: The Anger and Stress Management Book (2001)

Surviving and Thriving in a Blended Family (2000)

Teaching Children Patience Without Losing Yours (1999), with Polly Wilde

Hot Stuff to Help Kids Chill Out: The Anger Management Book (1997)

Treating Anger, Anxiety and Depression in Children and Adolescents: A Cognitive Behavioral Perspective (1996)

Anger Management in Schools: Alternatives to Student Violence (1995)

Rising Above: A Guide to Overcoming Obstacles and Finding Happiness (1995)

Rational Counseling with School Aged Populations: A Practical Guide (1992)

In addition to books, Dr. Wilde has written articles appearing in professional journals such as *Elementary School Guidance & Counseling, Journal of Cognitive Psychotherapy,* and *The Journal of Rational-Emotive and Cognitive-Behavior Therapy.*

Dr. Wilde presents workshops on subjects such as anger management, management of difficult behaviors, and cognitive-behavior therapy with children and adolescents. He and his wife, Polly, live in Richmond, Indiana, with their children, Anna and Jack.